Walking the Faery Pathway

(Includes the 'Faery Caille, Oracle of Wands')

*for Tom and
Sylvie
and the Faeries
around and in
the Roundhouse.
with
Love*

First published by O Books, 2009
O Books is an imprint of John Hunt Publishing Ltd., The Bothy, Deershot Lodge, Park Lane, Ropley,
Hants, SO24 0BE, UK
office1@o-books.net
www.o-books.net

Distribution in:	South Africa
	Stephan Phillips (pty) Ltd
UK and Europe	Email: orders@stephanphillips.com
Orca Book Services	Tel: 27 21 4489839 Telefax: 27 21 4479879
orders@orcabookservices.co.uk	
Tel: 01202 665432 Fax: 01202 666219	Text copyright Harmonia Saille 2008
Int. code (44)	
	Design: Stuart Davies
USA and Canada	
NBN	ISBN: 978 1 84694 245 7
custserv@nbnbooks.com	
Tel: 1 800 462 6420 Fax: 1 800 338 4550	All rights reserved. Except for brief quotations
	in critical articles or reviews, no part of this
Australia and New Zealand	book may be reproduced in any manner without
Brumby Books	prior written permission from the publishers.
sales@brumbybooks.com.au	
Tel: 61 3 9761 5535 Fax: 61 3 9761 7095	The rights of Author Name as author have been
	asserted in accordance with the Copyright,
Far East (offices in Singapore, Thailand,	Designs and Patents Act 1988.
Hong Kong, Taiwan)	
Pansing Distribution Pte Ltd	
kemal@pansing.com	A CIP catalogue record for this book is available
Tel: 65 6319 9939 Fax: 65 6462 5761	from the British Library.

Printed by Digital Book Print

O Books operates a distinctive and ethical publishing philosophy in
all areas of its business, from its global network of authors to
production and worldwide distribution.

Walking the
Faery Pathway

(Includes the 'Faery Caille, Oracle of Wands')

Harmonia Saille

**Cover Image and Black & White
Faery Illustrations by Demelza Hillier**

BOOKS

Winchester, UK
Washington, USA

CONTENTS

Dedication

For all the smaller members of my family (all girls), my younger stepdaughters Tanya and Joëlle, my granddaughters Holly, Elizabeth (Libby) and Tyler-Jean, my foster granddaughters Chloe and Emma, and my niece Lucy and great-nieces Libby, Carmen, and Harry (Harriet).

May their lives be filled with magic.

Acknowledgements

So many to thank but here we go. Thank you first to my husband Rick and to my children, stepchildren and grandchildren for all their patience, humor, support and faith. My grateful thanks go to my stepdaughters Tanya and Joëlle for their wonderful knowledge and thoughts.

Thanks to Mum for telling me about Uncle Bill, and Uncle Bill of course who didn't disillusion me. Thanks for all the memories go to both Mum and Dad (now both sadly deceased) for providing all the traditions and magic of my childhood. And thanks to Aunty Greba and Aunty Eileen and also to Mum and to my stepfather Gaz, all who contributed in my childhood lessons in wildflowers (a mixture of folk names, superstitions and identification) the interest in which has always remained with me. Thank you to all of my family and extended family. Grateful thanks goes to my sister Francesca Edge for her input on faeries and children and to Lucy too. Thanks to both of my sisters Francesca and Diane (Marelli) for all those lovely childhood games and nightly tales, especially Di for letting me be the handmaiden to her faery queen instead of the witch (sorry Fran).

My heartfelt thanks go to Beryl and Kerrie Weston for their inspiration and belief and also to my good friends Kaddy Parker, Ellen Knoops, Maria Zingoni and Russell B. Ashton (also for his photo of Stonehenge), for their support.

Thank you to all those people I spoke to in Irish pubs whose names I do not know, and also the lovely Janet Farrar and Gavin Bone, who talked to me about the *Bean Sidhe* and other faery phenomena.

Kimi Connell you are a star, thank you for the Southern Hemisphere festivals.

Thank you to Daniel Citynski for suggesting that gnomes or kabouters deserve a bigger place in books than they are usually given and suggested a wonderful Dutch book, which my husband Rick had also prompted me to buy a while before, which I failed to do!

Thank you to dear, dear friend Dr. Edmund Cusick (sadly also no longer with us) for introducing me to the dowsing rods and along with Dr. Jenny Newman taught me so much about writing.

Thank you indeed to Rhiannon Holbrook (aka Maggs/Seph) for her report on the faery she saw. And another thank you goes to Hedge for using text on the faery sighting from her forum and to all at White Wicca for their support.

Very, very special thanks to the lovely Demelza Hillier for the wonderful illustrations.

Introduction

Kerrie, a fey and intelligent young lady, said to me with total wonder and honesty in her beautiful eyes and a with huge smile lighting up her pretty face, 'We don't care what other people think. We believe it, don't we! We know they are real. We know they exist!' She was talking about faeries.

Wife of Bath's Tale (one of the Canterbury Tales)
Now in the olden days of King Arthur,
Of whom the Britons speak with great honour,
All this wide land was land of faery.
The elf-queen, with her jolly company,
Danced oftentimes on many a green mead;
This was the old opinion, as I read.
I speak of many hundred years ago;
But now no man can see the elves, you know.
For now the so-great charity and prayers
Of limiters and other holy friars
That do infest each land and every stream
As thick as motes are in a bright sunbeam,
Blessing halls, chambers, kitchens, ladies' bowers,
Cities and towns and castles and high towers,
Manors and barns and stables, aye and dairies-
This causes it that there are now no fairies.
For where was wont to walk full many an elf,
Right there walks now the limiter himself
In noons and afternoons and in mornings,
Saying his matins and such holy things,
As he goes round his district in his gown.
Women may now go safely up and down,
In every copse or under every tree;
There is no other incubus, than he,

And would do them nothing but dishonour.
Geoffrey Chaucer
(1340?-1400)

The lines above begin the tale of the Wife of Bath which was set long ago in the days of King Arthur when faery queens and elves where once common, and the jolly company often danced in the green meadow. The tale goes on to tell us how nowadays it is holy men that are common, and it is they who now walk where the faeries used to walk. In fact, the holy men infiltrate every corner of our world. They are on the land and in the streams, in the halls and chambers, and even in the barns and stables. At the end of the tale, Chaucer relates how the holy men chased away the faery folk and as a result women can now walk safely.

The irony of this tale begs the question 'at what cost do women now walk safely?' 'Holy men' is a metaphor for religion, but in modern times we can add 'science' to this, for sadly it was not just the faeries themselves that were chased away, but the belief in faeries, the living mythology and the magic.

Centuries ago, encouraged by religion and eternal damnation, people became afraid of magical and mystical things, though they still existed for them. In modern times, arriving in the seventeenth century with the *Enlightenment*, the scientific revolution has made a fair job of explaining away any strange and wonderful phenomena, and in turn Christianity itself suffered.

Many people believe that not everything can be so easily explained away. People see the impossible and the invisible — even people who were previously skeptical.

Carl G. Jung the eminent psychologist taught us many things about the psyche, believing that not everything can be systematically explained. He taught us about synchronicity (meaningful coincidences) and about the conscious and unconscious mind. The poet and artist William Blake regularly saw spirits, angels and faeries, and this ability was reflected in his work.

My own belief was always there. I was brought up by creative parents who believed children should have magic, imagination, and creativity in their lives — and rightly so. Is it any more fantastic to believe that faeries exist than spirits or ghosts and guardian angels? Many people, including many members of my family, have seen spirits during their lifetimes. Spirits exist on another dimension as do the faeries, and in Ireland faeries are often thought to be the spirits of the dead.

My own ancestry is from Ireland on my father's side and during her younger years, my mother and her family were brought up on the Isle of Man. My stepfather's family is Welsh. All these places have a wealth of folklore, magic and mystery attached to them. Belief was not totally wiped out in these and similar places, particularly Celtic areas, and so there are still more modern-day faery sightings to be found there than anywhere else. Faery folk are more open to people who believe in their existence.

Personally, I can see no reason why faeries, holy men, and indeed men of science, cannot now live happily side by side. Each has their own special place and to accept this is to open your mind, heart and spirit. There really is more out there for those who really look. There is so much to be discovered by those who really seek.

About This Book
This book is a guide to the faeries and their world but primarily it suggests ways to communicate with them. Although you will read about where faeries live and where you can find them, it is not a dictionary of faeries though I have included profiles of the various faery species of Europe and Scandinavia.

For me faeries are as real as you or I, helping me on many occasions, granting my wishes and giving me hope. I only ask for help in times of real need, and never ask for too much or the impossible. If you form a connection with the faeries as I have, then you can also gain much from this, and not just in the assistance you may request from them, but in bringing some magic into your life and bringing you closer to nature.

You might well ask now, 'so where do we find faeries and how do we contact them' and 'which ones do we contact?' In the following chapters I will explain how to find faeries and who to contact as well as who to avoid, for not all faeries are friendly. I will show you where to find faery leys, paths and gateways in your area, and why these are important. Additionally, for those who find it difficult to go out seeking faeries, I will guide you in how to attract them to your home and garden.

To solely learn faery names or types is not enough to gain a good connection with them. Many young children gain a connection by simply 'knowing' in an innate way that is often lost to us or driven out of us, as adults. In their magical world it does not occur to them that faeries do not exist. When we are older we need to gain some of the magic back to recapture that simple faith.

Gaining knowledge of the world of faery is paramount to connecting. By learning about their world you will come to respect them, and respect is crucial when dealing with them. Becoming familiar with faeries and their way of life will also add to your chances of a strong connection. I hope this book will bring you some way in gaining that knowledge and familiarity.

I was once talking to my mother about my interest in faeries and that is when she told me about Uncle Bill. When Uncle Bill was about ten years old and living on the Isle of Man, he was walking down a lane and heard strange irate voices coming from over a hedge or hill. He looked over and saw two faery men having a quarrel. My mother described them as knee high in height. Faeries often reveal themselves to children. Consequently — as it is also important — I will show you how to share this with the children in your life and how you in return can learn from them. Many children are growing up in a world that exists purely of technology and scientific facts, and all at the expense of imagination. And yet, imagination and creativity walk hand in hand. Albert Einstein is reported to have said, 'If you want your children to be intelligent, read them fairy tales. If you want them to be more intelligent, read them more fairy tales' (though there are variations on this). As the adults, it is our responsibility to provide or bring the magic into their lives.

If we as adults wish to become closer to the faeries, there is no one closer to them than our children. Your children will find it easier to contact and communicate with faeries than you will, so it as well to observe them.

Throughout this book you will read dialogue from my two stepdaughters Tanya (aged 11) and Joëlle (aged 9). The purpose of which is this. Many children are uncluttered by science and are lucky to have loving parents and family around them who ensure they keep the magic of childhood. As a result nothing is impossible for them. You would be surprised at what some children already know about faeries if you were only to ask them, like I did. Most of their knowledge is amazingly accurate and often comes from books, films and television, but significantly some is what they themselves believe or simply just know. If we can learn to accept this, then we can learn something from them.

Included in this book is *The Faery Caille, Oracle of Wands*. This faery tree oracle has more than one purpose. Similar to many other oracles it will help you in your everyday life and with everyday problems, and will guide you on future pathways. Additionally, the oracle will help you to communicate with the faeries and to become familiar with the trees that are sacred to them.

This book is not a short cut to knowing faeries but will certainly speed you on your way and assist you in becoming closer to them.

You will see I mention Celtic festivals on many occasions.

These are explained more fully at the end of the book.

My sincere apologies go to the 'little people' or 'good people' for lumping them all together under the one term 'faeries'.

Chapter 1

The Faery World

On where faeries live

Joëlle (aged 9): Faeries probably live in peaceful woods and forests. Why do people cut trees down? Faeries live in them.

Tanya (aged 11): Or they live in mushrooms like the Kabouter (a Dutch gnome).

Joëlle: Some faeries live in a house like a round circle with spikes on it, but it also has flowers and fun things.

Tanya: Faeries can live in a house like us. In fact the same house as us...in dark spaces.

Joëlle: I don't think so. I think they sleep in nature, not in real houses.

Tanya: If I were a faery, I'd prefer to live in a house because there's food everywhere. You can go into people's gardens instead of nature.

On language, size and shape-shifting

Joëlle: Faeries have their own language and can speak any language.

Tanya: Faeries are all different sizes.

Joëlle: Dwarfs are that big (knee high) and giants are twelve foot.

Tanya: Giants are sky high!

Tanya: Faeries can be our size, because sometimes you see people but they're faeries, you just never know. And they can be shape-shifters. In the community of humans they shape-shift into someone, into people.

Joëlle: Anything...an object...flowers!

Tanya: If you are walking past one and they don't want you to see them, then they change into a flower in the grass or something.

Joëlle: But they can also turn invisible.

Tanya: They can turn into animals if they want, like a cat or dogs and mice, and birds because they would want to fly away...or an owl because they like to fly at night.

Joëlle: They can shape-shift into teeth.

Tanya: Teeth!

Faery folk do indeed come in all shapes and sizes from the diminutive winged sprites, to human sized, or bigger. They live in a variety of places, inside — even in the human home — or outside in nature. Faeries can also be shape-shifters. I am not sure about them shape-shifting into teeth though, but you never know!

Some faeries appear to have been around for centuries upon centuries, while others are relatively new to the scene such as the tiny winged *Tinker Bell* look-alikes, who seem to have made an appearance less than two hundred years ago. Still, there many recorded sightings of winged faeries during this time. Many people believe these winged sprites are what constitute the faery and do not consider any other type, and yet it is actually the wingless faery men and women that over the centuries were most frequently sighted.

I have my own theory as to why winged sprites made such a late appearance. One reason why faeries make fewer appearances is perhaps because fewer people believe in them. Therefore these days when they do appear it is sometimes as the tiny winged sprite, perhaps to make it easier for us to accept them. This theory fits in with what the children say about faeries taking whatever shape or size pleases them. Alternatively, perhaps this type of faery just did not make an earlier appearance for one reason or another unbeknown to us.

Faeries are often categorized into groups.

On the earth itself or under the ground live the earth faeries, and among them are gnomes, leprechauns (an elf-like creature found solely in Ireland), and dwarfs who originated from Scandinavia along with the light and dark elves that have their own lands.

Belonging to the air or sky are the beautiful and ethereal sylphs and winged faeries. When the sky is painted with cirrus cloud, the wispy fluffy clouds set high in the sky on a clear or

summer's day, you might see the sylphs disguised among them. They also love to glide on the breezes and soar on the spiraling thermal air.

In the sea, rivers and waterways, and often in magical realms, live the various species of merfolk. Among these are the fish-tailed mermaids often seen combing their beautiful long hair, along with the striking Merrows of Ireland who have ugly men folk, and the Selkies of Scotland. The abode of merfolk is not only the sea but the lakes and rivers too. Not all merfolk have fish tails. Some are ugly, more usually the men, while others are strik-

ingly attractive. Merfolk often have powers of healing and some marry into the human species. More sinisterly, some merfolk particularly those of the sea are said to lure unwary folk to their deaths.

Trees sometimes have their own resident faery called a dryad, though there are other tree spirits that could be classed as dryads. Dryads prefer oak trees, while the elder tree has its own exclusive dryad, the Hyldemoer. The Gille Dubh or *Ghillie Dhu* is a Scottish birch tree dweller, and the Meliae are associated with the ash tree which you can read more about in the *Faery Caille* in Chapter 7.

All trees, however, are sacred to the faeries and Tanya was well to ask, 'Why do people cut trees down? Faeries live in them'. Care should be taken not to overly disturb trees, and taking saplings from the forest to plant in your garden is unacceptable. Moreover, think twice before cutting down any tree on your property as you could be cutting down a faery's home. And never dig up or move a hawthorn tree, if you want to avoid faery reprisals.

Trooping faeries are groups of faeries who travel the roads and faery pathways, especially at those certain times of the year when the veil between the worlds is thinner. Samhain is one of these times as is the Summer Solstice, (you can read more about these Celtic festivals at the end of the book). These processions are known as *Faery Rades* and the faeries are frequently seen riding horses or levitating. Many recorded instances tell of country folk coming upon a rade which would strike fear into their hearts. They would dive for cover in case harm or bad luck should befall them. Some rades are solemn especially in the case of a faery funeral as faeries are not immortal. Other rades are jolly affairs perhaps of celebration, and have music and raucousness, with faeries dressed in brightly colored clothing.

A faery tribe of Cornwall, the Spriggans are trooping faeries as are the German dwarfs and possibly the light elves and the Tuatha dé Danann of Ireland. Trooping faeries can be kind, malicious, or just plain tricky, and are of all different heights from tiny to human size.

The solitary faeries, as the name suggests, are faeries that travel alone. The malicious Duergar, the tricky leprechaun and the enigmatic tree dryad come into this category along with the Púka, Fir Darrig (various spellings), Bean Sidhe and the house faeries. However, the solitary faeries can still be social creatures, living or working close to each other. They make their homes in a variety of places, and you may find them in rocky mounds, holes in the ground, in trees, old mines, caves and in our own homes.

Faeries generally do like to live in the open, and construct their homes just about anywhere, forests and woodland are popular as are faery mounds or raths, and marshland or Irish bogs, though these homes are invisible to the human eye.

Some faeries make their homes in among humans in inhabited and uninhabited buildings. Some choose to live in old ruins and derelict buildings, castles, churches and monasteries, houses and cellars. You might also find them in the places where holy men 'now walk' as mentioned in *The wife of Bath's Tale*, outdoors in the lands and streams, and among humans in the halls and chambers, and the barns and stables, though nowadays they are invisible to us.

The Otherworld

Tanya: If Joëlle went into the faery world, for us it would be five minutes but for Joëlle it would be a long time...like in Narnia. If you go into the faery world, time stops here. But it can also happen that time stops there, and it goes fast here. You never know what will happen.

While aliens come from *outer space*, faeries come from *inner space*. The faery dimension called the Otherworld or faeryland is just beyond ours, in fact so close the faery can easily come into view, but these days, much to the chagrin of many, they choose not to and the reason is obvious. In the past, people simply *believed* and they would often see faeries. Nowadays, even when we believe, we perhaps try too hard when all we should be doing is encouraging the faeries to see we are friendly souls.

The Otherworld is a world that exists within or alongside our own earthly reality. Although it exists within and is parallel to our own earth, the Otherworld does not run in a simultaneous timeline. We cannot make a quantum leap from our own world to the faery world and always expect time to continue as it was from that moment on, for in the Otherworld time is a shifting time.

People who have strayed or were whisked away into the Otherworld and later returned to their own world have found one of the following three things: that their time there matches the time in their own world; that their time there, perhaps of many, many years, has only equaled a few days or even minutes in their own world; or and more often, it happens that a few days or even minutes in the Otherworld equals years in their own world. Additionally, tales have revealed that people who visit the Otherworld often lose all interest in life on their return.

The Otherworld or faeryland is the land of the faery folk. Imagine a beautiful place of emerald green fields, natural meadows, dense forests, oceans, rivers, great lakes, islands, rolling hills and majestic mountains, a virtual heaven on earth. The Otherworld is a natural landscape, rather like our world would have been had it not been touched by human influences in the name of progress and modernization, with its densely populated areas and often polluting industry. Perhaps it is not surprising then that faery visits to our world are less frequent. Faeries have it the way it used to be. They ride horses not drive cars, they walk not catch a bus, and some like the sylphs fly, but not in airplanes like we do. In fact if you look at it in this way, you can see faeries live in a world similar to the one in which our ancestors lived. Faeries have kings and queens and they live in hovels, small houses and palaces. They argue and fight, and they play sports — bowls and hurling being favorite games.

The Otherworld appears to shift as areas of it over the centuries have been known to appear and disappear, especially islands. An Irish island of the Otherworld called Tir na n Og, the magical land of eternal youth said to be the favorite dwelling of the Tuatha dé Danann, is a place where time cannot be measured. Some folk say it can be found on the west side of Aran, off the coast of County Clare.

My firm belief is that the otherworld is everywhere, a whole world co-existing with our own, with areas appearing and disappearing, according to human contamination, for faeries exist all over the world.

On the best time to see faeries

Tanya: Faeries come very early in the morning or when it first gets light.

Joëlle: ...And at about 9 o'clock at night when it's getting dark.

Tanya: Fireflies are really faeries. In the daytime they look like flying bugs but at night time they are faeries in glow gear.

A curtain of powerful magical energy separates Earth and the Otherworld which is commonly called the veil. Sometimes, especially at certain times of the year the veil thins and it is during these times that faery sightings are at their most frequent. Another time faeries are seen is at twilight, which is at both sunrise and sunset, and at specific times such as midnight, especially if they accidentally or deliberately step through a rift in the veil on faery pathways or around gateways and portals. These times are what are known as 'tween times, and are the times that are 'in between', neither day or night nor one day or another.

The guided visualization in Chapter 3 is a protected walk on a faery pathway and not a crossing into the Otherworld itself. If you start with this it will help you become accustomed to visualization and if you want to go further, make sure you have plenty of tuition beforehand and feel very sure of yourself. For more experienced people there is a second visualization exercise in Chapter 5, which reaches more into the Otherworld.

Good and Bad Faeries

Tanya: I saw a film about good goblins and bad goblins. Not all faeries are good.

Joëlle: No, some aren't...probably the goblins.

Tanya: That's what most people think, but some goblins are good. You can't really judge a book by its cover, so you can't really judge the goblins. Just because one's bad it doesn't mean they all are. There's a couple of good ones in the film I saw. But if you go into faeryland some faeries can trick you and you can get stuck there and never see your family again. So not all faeries are good because you can be turned into a faery like in *My Sister the Changeling* (my own novel in progress), and sometimes even a bad faery.

Joëlle: But sometimes you can be changed into a good one because you join the army to fight against the goblins like in *The Changeling* story. You probably need something special to get back to your own world after you have helped them.

Tanya: If everyone was the same it would be boring, the faery world has good and bad just like our world. So you have different types of people and different types of faeries, it's about equal.

Tanya is perfectly correct in that faery behavior differs. Some faeries could certainly be termed good or bad, but perhaps that is too simple a description. All people can sometimes be bad or tricky without being evil, while others are indeed malicious. Others can be good and benevolent hardly putting a foot wrong. What we do know for sure is nobody is perfect. And so it is in the faery world.

Some faeries are without a doubt good, while others are termed evil or malevolent, and the ones in between perhaps termed as tricky depending on the circumstances. The problem is you might not know which are which. With faeries, it is always advisable to be cautious. In communicating with them, I always name the faery type I wish to contact.

Among the ones to watch out for is the Gwyllion faery race of Wales who appear to be the counterpart of the Ellyllon also of Wales who are much friendlier. The Gwyllion are ugly and malicious mountain faeries. Travelers should be on their guard so that this faery does not accost them or cause them to lose their way.

The Duergar is another faery likely to cause travelers to lose their way, and this malicious and solitary, dwarf-like faery can cause all sorts of untold mischief such as switching road signs.

The goblin is another malevolent and ugly faery. While the hobgoblin who has from time to time received bad press, is a little more congenial and can be helpful though occasionally likes to play tricks on unsuspecting people.

The Scottish Kelpie, which appears as a water horse and can be found in rivers, calls for vigilance as he can take the form of an old man in tattered clothing, and is known to attack horsemen and sometimes to tear them apart before devouring them.

The good faeries regard humans in a favorable light and can at times be generous, but in turn they expect to be treated respectfully. Faeries have been well documented as willing to assist humans in times of need. Elves in every culture are known to help humans often carrying out work for them. The Knockers of Cornwall are mine faeries who would assist the tin miners in finding the ore, and they achieved this by 'knocking'. Another helpful faery is the Scottish brownie. The Seelie Court of Scotland is a multitude of kind and generous faeries and stands in stark contrast to the Unseelie Court faeries, which are malevolent and appear to have no redeeming qualities.

The 'in-between' faeries, those that are good but can also be tricky, can number among them the pixies and leprechauns along with the Fir Darrig, who wears a red cap and coat and occupies himself playing practical jokes.

When dealing with helpful faeries be polite and respectful. Thank them for help and leave a simple gift, but do not go overboard with a profuse garbling kind of thanks and extensive gift giving, which may come across as insincere (and might give the impression you are expecting the same help next time, which may not be possible, or may not happen). The faeries will know you are grateful without you having to be over generous or gushing.

An unusual gift to give the faeries is to render a service. I took a walk in the meadow to thank the faeries for a request of assistance coming true. My dog Chogan ran ahead and found a plastic bottle that someone had dumped close to the path. He carried it with him throughout the walk and all the way home. I had just walked past a chocolate wrapper, so following his example I collected it on the way back also picking up one or two other items of litter I found, and disposed of them at home. I felt I was shown this way of giving thanks and returning a favor through Chogan, which was a better and more useful gift than I could otherwise have thought of leaving. That same day by coincidence, my friend Aradia told me this,

The other day I was walking along thinking about helping the faeries and when I turned onto the short wilderness path that leads up to my house, I saw a load of rubbish, and at the bottom of the hill was a plastic bag waiting for me! I believe this was the faeries way of getting me to litter pick!

Faeries prefer well-kept house and gardens (which for some of us can be a little easier said than done!). As nature is their garden, litter picking is a good way to help keep our (and their) environment tidy, as well as having the forethought not to drop litter in the first place.

I am sure there are other ways to thank the faeries than purely leaving gifts, and this we can teach to our children.

Age, Mortality, Clothing, and Looks
On faery clothing

Joëlle: Faeries wear plain colors...yellowish-green and brown.

Tanya: Green, bright colors, but any shade of green. Camouflage colors. And red, such as the dress and shoes and red hats for the men.

Joëlle: People say these fluffy flowers are faeries...you know, a seed with hairs on.

Tanya: They have flowers round their necks and heads, and they have long bodies with wings made out of flower petals.

Faeries wear clothes in much the same way as we do. Hats, coats, shoes, trousers, shirts, skirts and frocks are the traditional clothing of most earth faeries. Modern or miniscule faeries commonly wear clothing of flower petals and foliage.

Generally the traditional clothing varies from beautiful or colorful, to old, dull and tatty depending on the faery species.

Flower faeries wear colorful clothing of flower petals, while dryads sometimes have clothes made from or decorated with leaves. Faery queens and kings wear more colorful and beautiful clothing.

Merfolk with fish tails frequently wear little else, others wear iridescent clothing made from fish scales.

The traditional faery colors of clothing that crop up more than any other are green and red. The coat or general clothing is green and worn with a red cap or hat. Many of the male faeries wear these. Occasionally it is blue coats with the red caps or hats and the Dutch *kabouter* is said to wear these colors.

The Feeorin are Lancashire faeries (which are perhaps related to the Manx Ferrishyn) and wear green coats. The stereotypical leprechaun is usually depicted wearing emerald green but was previously sighted wearing other colors, but more about that later in faeries of Ireland.

Male gnomes have been reported wearing blue coats, but again tall conical red hats and many garden gnomes are dressed so. The malicious Duergar is said to wear a lambskin coat and moleskin trousers and shoes with a hat of green moss.

Some faeries prefer to go *au naturel*, or barefoot.

Are faeries immortal? Perhaps some species are, but not all. Sightings of faery funerals have been reported and in quite some detail. The general consensus is that most faeries are not immortal though they may live for hundreds of years.

Faeries can be beautiful or ugly, though it is commonly the woman who is beautiful and the man ugly especially among the merfolk. The old crone or hag can be ugly but at times is known to transform into a beautiful maiden, and the male light elves are as fair to look upon as the women. Winged faeries are generally pretty, while goblins, dwarfs, ogres, giants and trolls are not exactly known for their good looks.

Faery Workers

Tanya: Some faeries collect jewelry and gems. And make rings and things. They can also make shoes. Elves are about this big (indicates six inches) and they make *big* shoes.

Joëlle: Not that small, about twelve inches. Faeries heal people, like when a cat can hurt you and then if it licks you it can heal you.

Tanya: Cats can't! Beowulf (the family kitten) bit me and he didn't heal me. Unless they're faeries then they might. Beowulf would be a young faery, too young to heal you.

Joëlle: Faeries can guard the kingdom.

Tanya: And you get faery godmothers. Sometimes there are faery queens.

Joëlle: Sometimes there are 1000 queens in one kingdom. But you only need one to rule, so I don't know why that is.

Tanya: Because there's the queen and then there's the sister and the cousin and so on and they are princesses and heir to the throne, and that's why they say there's a 1000 queens. A whole family of girls!

Joëlle: Or there could be a couple of queens for nature, and another couple for animals, and the palace and so on.

Faeries do indeed work just as we do. Spinners, weavers, musicians, mine workers, metal workers, healers, farmers, house servants, and yes shoe makers can be counted among the faeries. Many faeries are industrious and in turn reward industry. They dislike sloth and untidy, messy people.

The dwarfs have long been known to be skilled metal workers, making weapons and jewelry, often infused with magical powers. Leprechauns are cobblers or shoe makers, and the Knockers of Cornwall, mine workers.

Faeries are happy to help humans with their work on farms and with spinning and even housework as long as they are well treated in return.

Faery Food

Joëlle: Faeries eat petals.

Tanya: No, because some faeries are flowers! Bee honey!

Joëlle: Nectar!

Tanya: Probably things that are poisonous to us aren't poisonous to them. Anyway, you should never eat food offered by a faery because you can never eat normal food again.

Joëlle: Or you can probably get very, very ill. It might not be good for you.

A young man on one of my workshops was shocked when I suggested faeries love cream and milk. 'But that's an animal product' he protested. He had presumed that as nature spirits, faeries must also be vegan.

Faeries do indeed eat all types of food, and frequently steal or borrow food from humans and so eat much the same things as we do. They may well eat nectar and honey, but are also known to have a strong liking for milk, cream and butter, oat and barley meal, and small cakes. Some faeries favor the silverweed root, which resembles a small buttercup with silver foliage. Particular faeries are partial to the odd nip of alcohol which they will steal from your table and meat too.

However, if you in turn venture into the Otherworld and eat faery food then you may become trapped there forever as there is many a tale about this happening to some unfortunate person.

Chapter 2

Faery Pathways and Portals

Tanya: Hallowe'en is the faery door, and the door opens on other certain days, like Easter.

Joëlle: Yes, in a book it says at special times of the year like Easter, sometimes there's danger in the faery world and the faeries have to go out into the human world to find a human to go and help them. That could be true, I don't know.

Tanya: It is true! You never know if you go into a certain tree if it's a doorway.

Joëlle: Actually, when you're asleep and you dream of faeries, you might be awake. And something happens and then you go back to sleep, and you think you just dreamt about being in the faery world, but it was real.

I walked down the pathway past the row of thatched cottages, up and along the side of the farmer's field, clambered over three styles and across two meadows to reach the woodland that edged the river near Milston. Stopping in the clearing at the old Beech tree, I left three crystals where the trunk divided and laid my cheek against the rough bark. After I had spoken to the spirit of the tree, I walked down a barely noticeable path to the right through the tangled undergrowth and bushes, a blue damselfly following me all the way. Sentient to my surroundings, there it was — a magical feeling. I let it sweep over me, and savoring it I walked on down to the River Avon. I put a crystal into the water to greet the water spirits and walked back to the trees and there spoke to the faery folk, as I have the most affinity with the land or earth faeries. I stood for a while, not counting time, just looking around me and soaking up the magic. I saw something flash between the trees, too big to be a bird or insect, but when I walked over, there was nothing there...a magical mystical moment. This was one of my favorite places in Wiltshire.

More recently I went on a planned visit with my husband to see what magic the *Bloedsteen* or Bloodstone in the forest at Kernham held. The stone is thought to lie on a ley line and is near Ede in The Netherlands. I hoped to find magic there as I had in Wiltshire. The path leading up to the Bloodstone was mystical, the light was dim and rain fell. The thick canopy of trees

overhead cut out the light but sheltered us from the relentless rain. Now and then a large raindrop would drip from a leaf and fall heavily on top of our heads.

I slowly approached the stone which lay in the center of the path. My dowsing rods crossed as I reached it, indicating that energy was emanating from it. However, although the area was atmospheric, I did not have any feeling of magic and was disappointed. While my husband took photographs I wandered onto a carpet of sodden leaves down a narrow path through the trees to the right. As I reached a young oak tree I had an overwhelming awareness of magic. I stopped and looked around me. The feeling was the same, distinctly magical such as which rippled through me in the woods by the river in Wiltshire.

I walked on, but after a short while the magical sensation gradually dwindled. I walked back to the oak, and again there it was, that impression that something was here in this small area.

I took out my dowsing rods and picked up energy in a small area on the path and to the right of the path, again through tangled undergrowth and bushes. It was as if the faery folk watched the area from the undergrowth away from the main path. I greeted them.

This feeling I am describing is the one I seek when I go in search of the faery folk...the sensing of something there, of something magically mystical. Above all, this is the feeling I want you the reader to seek out and experience on your search for the faeries.

In past times, at twilight and at certain times of the year, it was advised to avoid likely gateways and portals to the Otherworld for fear of being spirited away. These gateways and portals are situated in ancient burial mounds or raths (hill forts), dolmens and stone circles, ancient ruins and monuments, or faery rings and faery pathways. Whether this happens in modern times as it used to in past times is unclear.

Faery Rings

A faery ring is a ring of mushrooms or toadstools which sometimes lies within a circle of darker or greener grass. Occasionally there are two circles of greener grass on either side of the toadstools.

Tales and folklore suggest you should never step into a faery ring, as the faeries will be angry with you. This is their territory. However with children it can be very different. When I was a child we had a faery ring beneath the old oak tree at the bottom of our garden. I would sit inside it with my two sisters and we would play our games of faeries and witches. We were not afraid, and our mother, who told us about the faery ring, never stopped us but would watch from the kitchen window. We never came to any harm.

Faery Pathways

If you have ever looked in a field and have seen a line of grass that is somewhat darker and richer then the rest, rather like with the faery rings, then this is a faery path and it could be faeries have trooped through there on their Faery Rades, or use it as a regular pathway. A faery path should never be built upon or obstructed. In Ireland there still exist stories of bad luck coming to those who do this, and constructors often check beforehand that they are not building on them.

If you look at it logically, to block a strong source of magical energy like this is courting trouble. Not only will it interrupt the course and the flow of energy angering the faery folk, but it will accumulate in your home or in the building in question bringing bad luck or illness to the occupant, even if the faeries decide not to curse you in the first place.

From the faery viewpoint, if someone was to decide to place a building on a public footpath you frequent, then you would not be happy about it.

From the human viewpoint if (by some ancient law) someone revealed that your home was accidentally built on a public footpath even if it only passes through your garden, which is sometimes the case, you would not take kindly to people traipsing through at any given moment of the day. The faery path would have the same, if not worse, effect on you, as the faery folk, although invisible to you, would disrupt your whole way of life with negative energies, as occasionally spirits do when haunting your home. So it is just as well to avoid building on faery paths.

Faery paths can also be ley lines, or any line that links ancient sites or faery raths. They can be called spirit paths, dragon lines, corpse roads or ways, coffin lines, lych ways and church ways. Many countries in Europe have these. In Germany they are known as the *geisterwege* and in The Netherlands the *dodenwegen* and *lijkwegen.*

Faery paths are not always ley lines, but can be, though perhaps it is easier to find a ley line than it is to find a faery field path.

Ley Lines

So what is a ley line? Ley lines were discovered by a businessman and inventor Alfred Watkins while out riding in 1925. His theory was that ancient sacred sites and features of the landscape appeared to be aligned. He recorded this in two books *The Old Straight Track* and *The Ley Hunter's Guide.*

So what constitutes an ancient site? An ancient site can by a natural though magical feature where worship took place, such as a hill or mountain, burial mounds or raths, standing stones,

old churches or cathedrals (sometimes built over more ancient places of worship), castles, ancient trees, lakes, crossroads, holy wells, or any other sacred feature in the landscape. One ley line in the UK passes through a church, hill fort, a holy well, abbey, the Cerne Abbas Giant (currently being re-chalked), and tumuli. Other leys pass through ancient stone circles such as Stonehenge and Avebury and though sacred sites such as Glastonbury.

Some folk do not believe in ley lines and have gone far in attempts to disprove them, though not so faery paths which have been around for so much longer. Ley lines exist as lines of energy, and most people who have traveled them can pick up on this energy by dowsing and also in a psychic or spiritual way.

I believe leys which can stretch from country to country — one stretches from the British Isles to the European Continent — is perhaps a way for faeries to magically travel, just as they travel along faery pathways, church way or spirit paths.

How to Find Ley Lines

You can conduct an internet search for ley lines in your area. Most countries have someone interested in them and have mapped them out. Otherwise take a map of your area that has historical, mystical, and ancient sites or landmarks, marked on it. An *Ordnance Survey* map could also be useful. You will need a ruler or straight edge, thread or string. Locate and mark the sites on the map and then see if you can trace straight lines between them. Some of the lines will pass on the edge of the site, but this is perfectly acceptable and the site can be counted. Some places you will find are very ancient, while others not so, perhaps only a few hundred years old. Circle all of these and then look to see how many line up. There should be no less than four that do but more often there is more. You may see that your ley includes a track, footpath or road, which could possibly have a more ancient origin.

You can use your divining rods to detect the energy when you

go to seek them out.

You will find instructions on how to make rods below.

Portals and Gateways

In this context, I personally refer to *portals* as an entrance to the Otherworld that has no fixed dimension. Think of Alice and the rabbit hole. A portal can be a wide area or a tiny hole, but like the rabbit hole it may take some time to pass through it and reach the Otherworld. When I refer to *gateways*, I mean an actual gateway or doorway which has a fixed point, although it too is an entrance to the Otherworld and you are immediately in the Otherworld once you walk through it. Portals and gateways can be found in ancient sites, particularly burial mounds or tumuli, and raths, as these are known to be entrances to the Otherworld. Stone circles are thought to be portals, along with trees, lakes hills and mountains.

Many trees have portals or gateways to the Otherworld. The three chief trees are oak, ash, and hawthorn. This triad of trees is a magical combination and a major portal to the Otherworld. The hawthorn protects the portal entrance. The elder, blackthorn, and alder are also said to be portals or gateways to the Otherworld. You can read more about these trees in the Faery Caille in

Chapter 7.
  When the veil between the worlds is thinner at twilight and on certain days of the year such as the Summer Solstice or Samhain, faeries pass easily through the portals and gateways and into our world.

Dowsing

I mention divining rods above. Divining rods are used for dowsing. Dowsing (also known as divining) is an ancient form of divination, and helpful in finding centers of energy. In the past, dowsing was seen as an agency of the devil, particularly by the Christian Church, though it is now generally viewed as being a scientific pursuit. Dowsing was and still is used to find water and minerals. Nowadays people use dowsing to also track ley lines and centers of energy at sacred sites, stone circles, and for some, even energy in their own homes. Others use dowsing as ways of finding lost objects, which works best if that object is linked to another one such as an earring. One earring can be held in the hand while the dowser dowses or divines a map or plan for the other. For this a pendulum is used.

MAKING DIVINING RODS

Some people think dowsing is the gift of a few. However, with enough practice and patience, anyone can learn to dowse. You can buy dowsing rods or make your own. The first dowsing rods I used were homemade and belonged to a friend and as soon as I picked them up I had a reaction which startled us both.

To make a set you will need a wire coat hanger and wire cutters. Cut rods from two coat hangers and bend them into an L

shape. I would suggest a length between twelve and sixteen inches for the longer part, and the shorter part between four and six inches. You then place the shorter lengths (the handles), into empty plastic pen cases so they can freely swing. The bought ones I have are on the shorter side, but if you make your own you can choose the longer length.

You can use your dowsing rods to detect energy centers and lines near you. Hold the rods loosely in your fists. You should be relaxed and your arms and the arms of the rods held out horizontally and parallel to the ground. Your elbows should be kept close to your body. Move forward slowly and keep relaxed. You will find that shortly the rods will begin to move around, without you doing anything to cause it. When they find an energy center, they will cross over suddenly or open out into a V shape.

Experiment by crisscrossing your paths, and be aware that your rods may be detecting water or power lines under the ground. I use the rods in places where I see energy, mists, or feel any strange vibes as well as on ley lines or at sacred sites. Using the rods can help you develop your psychic awareness as you can test any strange vibes you may come across.

Dowsing With A Pendulum

A pendulum hangs on the end of a chain or thread. You can buy a pendulum and there are many on offer, with some made of metal and some of crystal. You need to hold the end of the thread or chain with your index finger and thumb, holding it very steady so as not to influence the way it swings. Rest your elbow on a table to help keep it steady.

Generally you ask a question of the pendulum. Before using it you need to establish which way it swings for 'yes' and which way for 'no'. For me clockwise is yes and anti-clockwise is no. But it could be that for you swinging backwards and forwards is no and in a circular movement is yes. When I was young mother in the days before ultrasound scans, we used a needle and thread to establish whether someone pregnant was having a girl or boy by holding it over her stomach. A boy might have the pendulum swing in a straight line and a girl in circular motion. Again you would need to find out how it works for you first.

Putting It All Into Action

Now you know how to find energy, you might want to put it into action to try to discover areas that are likely to be faery pathways, portals or gateways. If you have had a mystical experience in a particular place then take your rods with you next time you go and see what you can detect. Take the rods to your favorite tree where you suspect a portal

or gateway lies, or to a rath, megalith, burial mound, or sacred site, which can be anywhere in the world.

With a pendulum, try dowsing a map of your area and ask questions about faery portals and pathways. You can later double check the area with dowsing rods or just by feel. By *feel* I am talking about the sense of magical energy I explained about earlier. If you think you have never experienced this, think about those times you were spooked by something, had a feeling someone was following you or was in your home, or that the phone was about to ring. A magical feeling can also be instantly recognized.

Chapter 3

Communicating with the Faery Folk

Ah, you open straight into fairyland, and the fairies love you and they will never change. Fairyland's always been there; it always was from the beginning of time and always will be to the end.
Henry James

I lay in my bed and suddenly I was aware of something hovering over me. I opened my eyes and saw what I can only describe as a sylph. She was a childlike ethereal spirit with long flowing hair, and she was elongated as she trailed off into nothing. She took me by the hand out of my body and we flew through the window and directly onto another plane.

The sylph kept hold of my hand and every so often turned to me to make sure I was all right. We flew over the most wonderful and magical land. For me it resembled the British countryside, except there were no houses, no people, nothing of the human influence. The color I most noticed was the vivid emerald green of the grass and trees, and the pure azure blue of the sky. It was tranquil and heavenly. I was relaxed, happy and contented, knowing I was privileged to be there. We did not see any other being.

We flew over forest, hill and dale, mountain and rivers, high in the sky looking down at the beauty. At last I realized I was somewhere not many people are lucky enough to go to, I was on another plane, a spiritual plane in another realm. The sylph looked at me though her face was indistinct. She had read my thoughts and seeing I knew where I was she nodded and let go of my hand and flew off into the distance.

I continued alone to fly around for a while, soaking up the beauty, knowing that one day perhaps I would visit there again, perhaps not until I died. This spooked me a little and so not wanting to overstay my

welcome, I decided to go back to my earthly body.
I opened my eyes stunned by the experience.

Astral travel is not strange to me as I have naturally done this for almost as long as I can remember, beginning somewhere between five and seven years old. The Sylph appearing was totally new to me, as was the experience of traveling onto another plane.

There are two ways to meet or communicate with faeries. One is through direct contact and the other psychically. If you cannot see faeries, which is the case with most people, one of the simplest ways is to go outdoors where you can experience Nature at her best and speak directly with the faery folk. Personally I cannot think of any better approach than to do this. Another way to communicate is through meditation and visualization, which is useful for those who live in cities, confined to their homes, or cannot easily reach countryside or parks.

Direct Contact

Tanya: We can see the faeries by communicating with them. You can leave them things like nectar or honey.

Joëlle: Or leave them food.

Tanya: We give them gems, because say they have a queen who has a big jeweled ball, they [the faeries] would keep adding more and more gems. They chip some off each one we leave, or take the spirit of the gem. I found a tiger stone on a beach and I climbed up a tree in the forest and I stuck it into a hollow in the tree. Then I saw lots of bumps just like there was a little city in the tree. And there were tiny bugs jumping about. If you put a magnifying glass on them you can see they're faeries but for us they look so small they look like bugs.

Joëlle: You can talk to them like praying, but in a big circle, but ask them things.

Tanya: You can hug the tree. Or leave a message in the tree and if it blows away it was just in the wrong tree and now it's going to the right one. If you ever find it again it will have very small writing on it and you'll need a magnifying glass to read it.

Joëlle: There was Tinker Bell the faery.

Tanya: You have to say 'I believe in faeries' —

Joëlle: — because if you do then they don't die. You have to believe in them. If you don't then one will probably die. You have to believe in faeries to see them. Sometimes you can see them, sometimes you can't.

Tanya: If you really, really want to see them, all you have to do is look. If you see an oak tree, put a gem in there and the next day if it has a chip you know they are there. Sometimes they need it, sometimes they don't.

Joëlle: You don't need proof.

Tanya: Some people think you have to see something to believe it, but you don't have to. You should try to be natural and you're more likely to see faeries.

As I have mentioned earlier it is better to name the faeries with which you would like to communicate.

For practical matters I ask the earth faeries. Gnomes, dwarfs, light elves, in fact those faeries known to have helped people. Anything to do with home, financial situations, career and projects can be included.

With the water faeries it is a little trickier, as water faeries can themselves be exceedingly tricky. I generally address the *good faeries of the water*, in matters of the emotions, such as the heart. They can also be of assistance in matters of health.

Consult the faeries of the air on matters of the mind, knowledge and writing skills. Anything to do with studying and spiritual matters can also be included.

Elemental faeries of the fire can be consulted for those matters buried deep in the subconscious and which often materialize as fears, and also those matters that require strength, energy and creativity. Fire keeps us warm and can light the way, so in matters needing direction, the fire faeries can also be helpful.

In *The Faery Caille, Oracle of Wands* I discuss communication with faeries through trees. Faeries are very much connected with nature and especially with trees. Communication should take place in outside whenever possible. If you wish to talk to the fairies choose somewhere such as the countryside, park, garden, riverside or ocean. Find a particular tree in your neighborhood, perhaps one you can return to regularly.

You do not have to talk aloud but through telepathy. This also helps to prevent you becoming known as the local eccentric who talks to faeries and trees (although most people smile indulgently if they see you hugging a tree).

Never ask for too much or the impossible. I would class winning the lottery as the impossible. Ask for help in times of real need for yourself and others. Do not feel guilty for asking for personal help as there is nothing wrong or selfish in this. But do remember the old adage 'be careful what you wish for'.

Please do not take the faeries for granted and do remember to talk to them when you are not in need even just to say hello and acknowledge their presence. You would never ignore a friend you met on a path just because you have nothing to ask of them, this would be far from polite.

Tanya and Joëlle have given tips on how to communicate with

faeries. You can leave small gifts in trees or throw them into the sea or river. Faeries like to have food gifts such as honey and cream. Small gems or sparkly gifts are also favored. Pick up litter around the place where you communicate with them.

There are more tips in the *Faery Caille* in Chapter 7.

Exercises for the Senses

Oh, do not tell the priest our plight,
Or he would call it a sin;
But—we have been out in the woods all night,
A-conjuring Summer in!

From *A Tree Song*, Rudyard Kipling

Faeries love nature and nature loving people. If you do not already, learn to love and appreciate nature. Begin by going outside even if it is just in your garden, a park, or in the countryside. Take someone with you if the area is not safe to walk alone. Take a child with you too. Children are wonderfully innocent and they might see things that you miss and will help keep you focused.

This exercise is for inland nature, but if you live near the ocean then you can go there and substitute what is below for all the sights, sounds, and smells you will find there. I have given a few tips for this.

In this exercise you need to use all your senses; seeing, hearing, voice, smell, touch, and intuition. Nature is not passive it is active, moving, mutable, always offering something new to see. Watch the seasons change, wherever you are there will always be some changes, climate changing, buds opening, fruit ripening, leaves turning. You will be surprised at how much you ignore nature's sights, sounds and smells. If you ignore nature then you ignore faeries. If you never see nature, then you will never see faeries. If you do learn to see nature, after a while you will wonder how you did not see it all before.

1. Teach yourself to 'see'. Look upwards to the sky. Is the sky a clear azure blue or are there clouds? Are the clouds downy white or gloomy gray? Are they the high wispy cirrus clouds, or the lower fluffy cumulous clouds? Imagine sylphs and winged faeries gliding and soaring among them on the breeze. Is the rain falling? Is it a gentle or sharp shower or violent stormy rain? Do you see birds? If so, do you recognize what they are? Try to pick one out and then look it up in a book or on the internet. Look around you, are there any trees? What trees are they, again pick one out, and take a leaf for later identification. If they do not have leaves, look at the buds or texture of the bark. Some trees have the most wonderful bark with intricate patterns. The silver birch has silvery-white bark, and the willow has an amazing bark with deep fissures. And let us not forget the wonderful camouflage or mottled bark of the mighty sycamore tree. Do you see any flowers, particularly wildflowers? Note their color and take a photograph for later identification. Do you see bees and butterflies and other insects, perhaps ants or beetles? Do you see damselflies, dragonflies, herons or ducks on a pond or lake, or a fish leaping? Do you see a hare tearing across the plain, or a squirrel running up a tree? When you are out walking you will be surprised at how much more you will see in nature then you do now. Instead of letting your thoughts wander, sometimes stressful thoughts, you will actually see what is around you. Seeing is a therapy in itself as you will learn to enjoy your walk and will become thoroughly relaxed.

If you are by the ocean look for something swimming in the sea, a dolphin or seal, or flying above it, a seagull, or pelican, or on the ground a crab crawling on the golden or white sand. Look for foam on the waves or reflections on the water. Watch the sun rise or set, a most spectacular sight.

2. Learn to 'hear'. Listen out for bird song, bees or other insects buzzing. Listen out for animals crying or growling. Listen to the wind rustling or whispering, or howling through the trees, and the leaves, cones, chestnuts, or nuts falling. Listen for the rain spattering, a brook tinkling its merry tune, or a river rushing. Listen for fire crackling.

   If you are by the ocean, listen for the crashing of the waves or the screech of the gull as he swoops down to capture a fish. Put a sea shell close to your ear and hear the sound of the ocean.

3. Teach yourself to notice scents. Smell the scent of trees, blossom and flowers floating on the breeze, the wet freshness of grass after a shower of rain, a wood fire or leaves burning, especially in the autumn.

   By the ocean smell the saltiness of the sea air and the seaweed.

4. Use your voice. Hum or sing while you walk. Sit outside and play soft music or a musical instrument. Faeries love music. If you are in a cave, or enclosed area, or the top of a gorge, call out or sing, and listen to your echo come back. Talk to the trees.

   By the ocean choose a song of haunting music and softly sing to please the merfolk.

5. Learn to *feel*. Do not just touch, but *feel* the soft velvet of a rose or silkiness of the tulip. Watch out for stinging nettles.

Hug a tree and feel its energy, send out your love to it, faeries sometimes live in trees. Feel the rough or smooth bark. Feel the grass beneath you bare feet. If you have never run across a meadow or lawn in your bare feet, then you have been missing a wonderful feeling of freedom. Dangle your feet in a brook in the summer months, the water may be cold at first but you will get used to it. In the winter, put your hand in the water or skate on an outside pond as long as you know it is safe to do so (it may be prudent to ensure you are not alone). Feel the breeze or rain on your skin.

By the ocean, paddle or swim feeling the waves brush your skin. Walk barefoot and feel the wet sand ooze between your toes, or on dry sand the silky softness and let it run through your fingers. Feel the warming sun on your skin.

6. Practice your intuition. Intuition is something we all have. Use it more and it will develop and become stronger. Try to sense everything around you. Do you sense an animal

around? Or perhaps you get a particular feeling of something magical in a grove of trees, and know that this particular area is a special place, that perhaps faeries live in. Do you have an unexplained feeling when hugging a tree because you can feel its energy? Go out on your walk in anticipation of seeing something extraordinary and you just might.

By the ocean do you sense anything extraordinary? Watch, wait, and anticipate.

Visualization Exercise 1, *Walking the Faery Pathway*

Although you will find people who claim to see faeries, you are not a lesser person just because you do not see them yourself. And even if you never do, they are still around and can hear whatever you are communicating to them.

Of course there are still many recorded modern sightings of faeries and many people see faeries in ways other than directly, and that is in their peripheral vision. If you think you keep seeing something out of the corner of your eye then you probably are, so do not write it off as an 'it was probably nothing' moment. Another way is through astral travel. From one realm directly to the other we can speak with them or visit them. Not everyone can astral travel, but if you can, than this is one way of contacting the faeries and some people do.

If you do not astral travel or have shamanistic skills, one of the ways to see faeries is through visualization. Many people do achieve something with this. The more skilled you are at visualization, the more successful you will be.

The main skill you need for this is relaxation. Find yourself a quiet space where no one can disturb you. You can play some non-intrusive music or nature sounds. If you live in a noisy area, raise the volume of your music and wear ear plugs. Light some candles and incense to provide ambience and put you in a relaxed frame of mind. You will find a list of incenses and candle colors below (and a color guide at the end of the book).

In this visualization I will guide you to meet the faery folk. You will not go into the Otherworld. Instead you will travel a faery path where the veil between worlds is thinner. Try to do this exercise when the veil will be even thinner at Samhain, Bealtaine and the Summer Solstice, or at twilight or midnight on any day.

Do take with you a single glove or failing this an offering as you will need permission to walk the path. The best offering will be one you can comfortably hold in your hand or lie in your lap, while in total relaxation.

You can do this visualization inside or outside. You will not require the ambience if you have found yourself a lovely spot in a meadow, as the sounds of nature will suffice. But still have an offering ready.

If you are inside you can recline in a chair or sit on the floor. If you are outside and you have found yourself a tree, you can lean against the trunk; otherwise sit on the grass in a position which is most comfortable for you.

Suggestions for offerings

A glove if possible to throw down on the path otherwise –
A rose quartz crystal

Meditation incense and candles

Purple or white candles
Frankincense or sandalwood stick or cone incense

If you wish to make your own incense you will need to use a safe container to burn it in and a block of special easy-to-light charcoal available from New Age shops (this is not the same as quick lighting barbeque charcoal). You may want to ventilate your room if indoors, or if you suffer from asthma this might cause irritation. You can mix together a *selection* of the following ingredients available from New Age or health shops or even you own kitchen:

Frankincense (resin)
Sandalwood (oil can be used)
Mugwort (can be found at the side of roads, wasteland, or natural meadows)
Wormwood
Jasmine
Bay
Parsley
Lavender (oil can be used)
Chamomile
Poppy seed
Cinquefoil
Juniper
Yarrow
Any of the herbs above can be substituted for a few drops of essential oil.

Read the exercise several times to familiarize yourself with it. I deliberately did not make it too long and you do not have to remember it exactly.

After you have settled yourself down, spend a few minutes totally relaxing your body. Loosely hold the glove or crystal or place it in your lap. Shield yourself from potential harm by building a protective circle around you. Do this by concentrating on your powerful inner energy. This magical energy radiates outwards gradually from the solar plexus (deep inside you just below the breast bone) in the form of a blue light, it becomes denser as moving clockwise it forms a globe around you, and nothing can penetrate it. Watch it as it becomes brighter and stronger until you are sitting inside a globe of protection, around, above and below you. Now nothing can harm you. Take a few deep breaths to further help you relax.

To begin with and before starting your journey, imagine you are in a beautiful walled garden. The cottage garden is a tall mixture of flowers overcrowding their beds with cobbled paths winding in and out of them. Butterflies flit from bloom to bloom collecting their nectar, and there is a pleasant humming of bees. A sundial sits in the center of the garden and the wall itself is covered in honeysuckle and ivy. Before you is the great, black, iron gateway though which you will soon pass. When you are ready, begin.

The gateway has a large round ring handle. Use it to pull the gate open. This will take some effort as the gate is extremely heavy and old.

You step into a beautiful undisturbed meadow. The sun is bright in the azure sky, and the emerald grass is littered with colorful wildflowers. You can see margaritas, the bluest and biggest cornflowers you have ever seen, red clover and poppies, the purple knapweed, yellow vetchling, and pink and white milfoil. In the distance there is an undulating landscape of green fields of forty shades of green and a dotting of solitary trees and hedgerows here and there.

Take a walk through the meadow. As you walk take a deep breath and smell the sweet scent of the flowers, hear the buzzing of the bees and the songs of the birds, and watch the butterflies as they flit from flower to flower.

An iridescent green dragonfly hovers in front of you, it then flies off slowly, and every so often it hovers as if waiting for you. Follow it.

It leads you through the meadow and to a tiny brook. The water tinkles musically as it travels gaily along. Now follow the stream.

The stream leads you out of the meadow and into a field of lush grass. Ahead, you can see that at the edge of the field and stretching for miles, is a darker pathway of undisturbed even more lush grass of darker green. You walk towards it and away from the stream. Stop at the beginning of this path as it is the faery pathway and you will need permission to walk it. Throw down your glove or place your offering on the pathway (psychically) and wait a while. Watch and hear the grass move in waves as the breeze brushes it.

Suddenly the ground begins to tremble beneath your feet. Do not be afraid. The trembling becomes rumbling and you can actually hear it now. A crack appears in the ground in front of you. Stay where you are. Steam comes from the crack and then it opens into a hole and fire leaps from it, you can feel the heat but it does not burn you.

Out of the ground a fiery lizard appears. This is the guardian fire salamander of the pathway. You are still not afraid.

It sees your offering on the ground in front of you. It does not touch it but nods its head and sinks back into the ground. The hole closes and the steam disappears through the crack in the ground as it closes over, and you are once more alone.

You now have permission to continue.

Now you can step onto the pathway and continue on your way. As you walk along listening to the birdsong, you see a hawthorn tree. As this is a lone tree it belongs to the faery folk, so do not touch it. From behind the tree a small man appears. His face is wizened like crumpled brown paper. No more than knee high he approaches you. This is a gnome of the earth. Stop and listen to what he has to say. Does he give you a message?

If he does not speak to you then speak to him. Greet him, 'Good morning/afternoon/evening, Sir'. Wait to see if he speaks, if he does not, bow your head in greeting and say goodbye and walk on.

The path winds downhill now and you follow it until it eventually winds uphill again. When you get to the top, stop and wait.

Look up into the sky. You see a beautiful bird-like white creature, which is ethereal and childlike. It soars on the rising air streams. Seeing you, it begins to glide downwards towards you in ever decreasing circles.

Greet it as it comes within speaking distance. This is a sylph of the air.

Again wait for a message. If none is forthcoming nod your head and walk on.

As you walk the pathway, you hear the sound of the gaily traveling water. You come once more to the babbling brook. You stay on the pathway but walk alongside it.

Gradually the brook widens until it becomes a river opening out into the sea in the distance.

You stop and look at the water. Something is disturbing the surface of it. Suddenly a head appears; it is a beautiful head, with long flowing hair, and on it a cap of red feathers. It soon becomes apparent that this is woman. Her white arms reach out of the water as she surfaces. Her eyes are dark and mysterious. You see webbing between her fingers.

Out of the water next to her a man surfaces. His skin, hair and teeth are of green. A long red nose and pig-like eyes do not help his ugly appearance. His arms are short and fin-like and he also wears a red feathered cocked hat. What you see of him is naked but he is a friendly fellow and can bring you luck.

These are the water merrow. Greet them but if you are male watch out for the wily female as she likes to tease mortal men and you may even become enchanted by her.

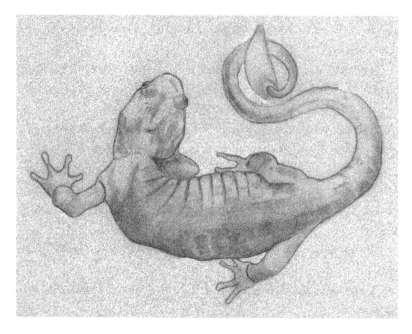

Again wait to see if they have a message for you. The message coming from the male merrow may be of good luck wishes, emotional or health matters.

Leave them now and turn and walk back to the meadow. Think about what you have seen. You might meet someone else on the way back, who do you meet, what do they look like, and do they give you any messages?

Finally, collect your glove from the ground and step off the path and remember to say goodbye to the faery folk and thank them. Pass once more through the meadow and open the great, iron gate to the walled garden.

Sit down on a bench by a flower bed and rest for a few moments. Take a few deep breaths and release the circle of protective energy, letting it sink back to your solar plexus. When you are ready open your eyes.

You have now greeted faery folk from all four elements of fire, earth, air, and water. You might not receive a message the first time you go. And next time you might well run into even more or different faeries.

Try just walking through onto the pathway, always leaving your offering at the start. Wait to see if you need permission, if you do, then something will appear and accept the offering. If nothing happens then you can safely walk on.

There is another exercise in Chapter 5 for those more experienced.

Chapter 4

Children and Faeries

Tanya: The kingdom of the tooth faery is very white because of all the teeth.

Joëlle: The king and queen are white too.

Tanya: ...Because of the white clothing.

Joëlle: The beds are all spiky, because they're made out of teeth.

Tanya: ...But they can put soft leaves on them.

Joëlle: The tooth faery must be strong to get under the pillows.

Tanya and Joëlle (In unison): We like the tooth faery because we get money.

Tanya: I wrapped my tooth in toilet tissue and Mum threw it away accidentally. She told me to write a note to the tooth faery to say what happened and to apologize.

Joëlle: And did you get the money?

Tanya: Yes.

Joëlle: Once my tooth fell out in the night. In the morning I noticed it was gone and checked my mouth but it wasn't there. I checked in the bed and on the floor but someone had picked it up already because I found it on the sink. I wrote a letter to the tooth faery saying I lost my tooth but someone found it — just in case she forgot me.

The fact that faeries often appear to children has been well documented. Yet children often tell us things that we as adults attribute to an active imagination. We perhaps all too readily dismiss what they say with an indulgent smile. What would happen if we accepted some of their stories as truth?

If this happens to you, then perhaps ask the child to describe any strange phenomena in more detail. If you do, bear in mind that the children may talk about things you would not expect them to know about. Try to be open-minded. If they say they have seen a faery for instance, I would suggest going with the child to see exactly where this appearance took place and share in it.

According to my sister Francesca, children are 'open books' who are naturally mystical and magical and have great imaginations. However, she says, it is what you do with your children that helps shape them. If you quash the wonder in their worlds, then they will let go of the magic. If you try to retain some of that magic in yourself then you will encourage your children to do so, and they will grow up open-minded to the hidden of the world. Francesca goes on to say that surely it is easier to retain some magic than to try to get it back or produce it later on in life. Our world is not just cold hard facts, but a wonderful place with hidden worlds which we can access. The open-mindedness of children causes them to naturally attach themselves to magical and mystical things like the faeries, as they have a keen curiosity. She goes on to talk about her youngest daughter Lucy who loves the faeries and sometimes feels she is one. Many of us have had such thoughts as children.

A teenager Rhiannon aged sixteen at the time, contacted me about a faery she saw in Wiltshire last year. She said:

I was on my way to Swindon to go to Avebury with a friend on the bus, and I chanced to look up this old path, and to my utter amazement I saw a little creature. Now I know there are really short people in the world, but I swear, it wasn't human, I could feel it! It was only about...2 ft tall! And it wore a raggy old hat, a long coat and it carried a stick that was about two inch higher than it's head...walking down the path. Now, I think the reason I saw it was because I was on my way to

Avebury to celebrate the summer solstice with my friend...and it's said that the boundaries between worlds are very thin at that time. But I assure you, I wasn't seeing things, I know I saw it, I felt it!

Children can be psychic and see things that we cannot. My own daughter had an imaginary friend and we had to set an extra place at the table for him. My friend's granddaughter Danielle also had an imaginary friend and asked my son to escort her to the bathroom. When they reached the top of the stairs, she said 'Don't go in the there,' and pointed to her grandmother's room, 'there's ghosts in there.' She was three years old at the time and her grandmother is a psychic who frequently sees spirits in the house but had never discussed this with her granddaughter. My eldest son, when he was only two years old was once with my parents and me when visiting a five hundred year old country house. We were walking up the narrow winding staircase and he suddenly said, 'There's ghosts in here.' We were astounded as we had never told him about or discussed ghosts before, neither was he yet at playgroup and he was the only child at that time. Another son once saw a child spirit, which I can confirm, as I also saw it the previous day but had not told anyone. My youngest son has seen spirits, ghostly furniture and orbs since he was five years old, and having just reached adulthood he still sees spirits, orbs, auras, furniture which is not there, and other strange phenomena. If your child has an imaginary friend, then do not discourage it as in time they just disappear. Often it is said these are spirits or faeries. If your child 'sees' things do not dismiss it as they are probably telling the truth. Many children lose this ability at puberty.

In past generations, stories of faery abductions and of faery sightings or meetings were passed down to the children commonly in the form of tales. Some of this oral tradition was owing to illiteracy. To hear of such stories nowadays the older generation can still be consulted especially in places where there is a strong tradition of folklore, such as Ireland. I have personally heard such tales and stories of faery sightings and experiences and not just from the older generation. For the future, there are luckily modern authors who still collect and write about faery sightings. The more modern *blog* can be a way of recording experiences. Whatever we do and how we record it, perhaps we should follow the example of previous generations and pass down stories of faery sightings to our own children so that recorded and oral accounts of them are not one day viewed as ancient history.

The same problem exists with our old traditions which are fading as they go out of fashion and new ones take their places. When I was young, Hallowe'en was a festival of apples, a night of 'duck apple' also known as 'bobbing for apples'. You seldom hear of anyone doing this now. Perhaps we should treasure the old traditions if they are not one day to become just a thing of the past.

Suggestions for Samhain/Hallowe'en

Samhain is a night of the faeries and the spirits. It is traditionally a night for children to have some fun too.

If like me you do not have young ones around anymore on the night of Samhain (Hallowe'en), then you can always invite the adults instead for some fun and get them to bring their own children. If you include leaving food out for the faeries you can attach great ceremony to this.

For traditional feasting fun, serve apples and nuts and provide mulled wine for the adults and fruit juice for the children. Bake potatoes in a fire and roast chestnuts and make some treacle toffee and toffee apples to give as prizes. For the faery folk leave gifts out at dusk and welcome them, so they too can join in the celebrations.

Stand at the door (to your garden if you have one or the

balcony of your apartment) and formerly ask the faeries to join in the festivities. Gifts can include a bowl of cream or milk. Little cakes can be baked and the children can join in with this. Gemstones can be left out too. This can also be done on Midsummer Night/Summer Solstice another night of the faeries. Leave a Jack O'Lantern or light a candle in the same place where you leave the gifts. When I was young the Jack O'Lantern was made from a swede (known as a turnip in some areas) and it was not easy to carve.

Try duck apple or bobbing for apples, especially if you have never done this before. Fill a large tub, an old baby bath or garden tub will do. Place several apples in it. Blindfold those taking part and they have to keep their hands behind their backs. The first person to pick out an apple with their teeth is the winner. Alternatively, tie apples to strings and the people can kneel and try to catch them with their teeth without use of hands. For adult or teen game suggestions, cut an apple in half across the middle (not through the stalk) to reveal the five pointed star. Think of five things in your life you would like to change. Contemplate those things for a while, and then eat the apple to help them come true. Alternatively, peel an apple and throw the skin over your shoulder to reveal the initial of the person who will become your future sweetheart.

Make a *Dumb* cake with fruit and nuts. The cake must be made by the unmarried in complete silence. Put a piece of the cake under your pillow to dream of the person you will marry. Putting a sprig of rosemary under the pillow achieves the same thing. Look in a mirror at midnight and comb your hair and eat an apple at the same time to see your true love's reflection behind you.

Throw two nuts in the fire if you are trying to choose between lovers. The first one to crack is the true one. On the other hand, if you throw two nuts in the fire to represent you and your lover and they burn long and slow together, then you will be happy. If one nut jumps apart from the other, you will not.

Encouraging Your Children's Imaginations

Tanya: We used to put gems in a tree, when we were walking in the woods you turn your head because you think you saw something out of the corner of your eye, but you think 'where is it' because there's nothing there.

Joëlle: It's like something is hunting you. Tanya: We saw something. We said what's there? Then we put gems in the river and the next day they had gone. Joëlle: When we were walking Chogan (the family dog) that day he was shaking his head all the time, he doesn't usually shake his head all about. He could definitely see something. Tanya: The faery must have been on his back, it's just that we don't see it. It only shows itself when it wants us to see it. It hides itself.

Joëlle: Or you can have things like a special glass or stone, and when you look through you can see something then. People who look in crystal balls work with leprechauns. They see things.

Tanya: I think cats can see faeries because they normally chase flowers. You know those flowers (dandelion clocks) that you blow and they chase them. And they're faeries aren't they. They try to keep away, because cats can jump up.

Joëlle: In the big field I always turn around when I see something, and think is that one of the cats.

Tanya: Yes, when we were on the big field, all the cats were inside, but we thought we saw cats, and behind us we could see something rustling in the grass but there was nothing there.

Joëlle: Sometimes the cats play with something but there's nothing there, they try to catch something. I wonder what that is.

The best way to encourage a child's imagination is to assist them with play. Too much time is spent on computers in this busy day and age, although they have their place. When I was a child, my mother would tip up the dining table for us children to use a boat, but I cannot see that happening these days as furniture is not stout enough for such rough use and far too expensive. I would suggest taking your children on a nature walk and let them talk you through what they see. Provide them with some little gemstones to leave in trees as a gift. Go on a specific faery hunt. Ask the children where they think the faeries are and stop at that place. When I lived for a short time too far from the countryside to walk there, we would walk in the park instead. The children had several favorite faery trees there, one of which was protected by railings and we would have to throw the gemstones and try to land them in hollow.

Provide art materials so the children can draw faeries. Help them to invent games. Read them faery stories, myths and legends. As long as it is safe to do so, let them run barefoot through fields. Alternatively, guide your children in making your home, garden or outside space a faery friendly area. It is possible for us all to have some magic in our lives. Bear in mind the wise words of Albert Einstein which I have recorded in the introduction, 'If you want your children to be intelligent, read them fairy tales. If you want them to be more intelligent, read them more fairy tales'.

Chapter 5

Faery House and Faery Garden

Faery House

Faeries, as we have learnt from our experts Tanya and Joëlle, live indoors as well as out. Here I have included a few extra ideas for attracting a resident faery, presuming you do not already have one.

There is a warning with this. House faeries can be tricky and play tricks on you. If you develop a bad relationship

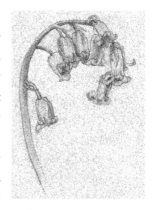

with your faery he might just decide he enjoys tormenting you and stays put even if you wish him to leave! So if you decide you would like a house faery, treat him well.

You will see I have called the house faery 'him' this is because most house faeries are male and of the elf species. I say *most* but not *all*, as I am sure there are faeries of either sex and it could be you see other types of faery in your house from time to time. They do come in sometimes, so do not be surprised if this happens. You might not always see them but they will make their presence known.

Tips for Attracting a House Faery

- Prepare a small dark but warm corner for your faery preferably a little away from your own seating area. Good areas are the kitchen, cellar, attic room, or just the corner of any room you have deemed suitable or the only one you can use. I would not advise to prepare space for him in your bedroom. He might keep you awake at night or vice versa.

- In the corner place a small table, or stool you can use as a table. If you feel you must, then make up a bed for your faery. As your faery will be about knee high, then you can use a small dog or cat bed with a doll pillow and blanket. (If people ask what it is, then tell them it is for your resident faery, they will probably not ask again). Of course if you have one, then your cat or dog may wish to sleep on it. Otherwise leave it as he may bring his own invisible bed with him, so make space for it.
- Play jolly music to attract your faery.
- Occasionally leave food and drink for your faery, and small gifts.
- A candle or lamp.
- Make a window box for him (instructions below in 'Faery Garden'), or if no window is near to his corner, leave a plant that likes the dark. Otherwise make a faery window box in the same room, or make a faery garden he can go out to visit.
- Hang a witch's ball in the window (made of glass and containing sand, feathers or glitter).

Tips for Caring for Your House Faery

- Once he has taken up residence find a name for your faery as it is not good to call him 'faery'. A name should magically come to you that he has put into your head, or perhaps you will come across this somehow, so look out for it. Try not to leave it too long or at least tell him you wish to know his name.
- As he will possibly have taken all he requires from a gemstone after a month, replace it with a fresh one.
- Refresh other gifts regularly and remember to always thank him for favors (not too profusely) and above all talk to him. Do not leave him clothing as he might be one of those faeries who resent this.
- If you go away on holiday, leave gifts and explain how long you will be gone. Your faery will help himself to food so do not worry too much. If he does not live in the kitchen, then leave the door open for him. Not that he needs it, but it is the thoughtful gesture that counts.
- Invite your faery to join in family and other celebrations.
- On special Celtic festivals, particularly Summer Solstice and Samhain, have a celebration for your faery.
- Play music for your faery. Jolly jigs are favored. Dance with him if you like.
- Above all else, respect your faery and give him space.

Faery Garden

All types of faeries might visit your garden. However, in more recent times it is more the small winged type that is sighted in gardens. Below I have suggested many things you can add to your garden or faery space. These are just suggestions and

you will probably form some ideas of your own.

Faeries love gardens have long been sighted in them, usually at the bottom. If you have space at the bottom of your garden then this is a good place to put your faery patch. Other ideal places are beneath or close to a tree. Close to water or a stream would be perfect. A water feature would be lovely. If you do not have one, then you can always make one. If at all possible, then place your faery garden away from the house. Any size is good even a small patch (see photo below). If you do not have a garden or yard, then you can make a window box (instructions below).

Things You Might Like to Include

- A small table or use a stool as a table on which to put a lamp, candle holder, offerings and gifts.
- Make narrow pathways between plants for the faeries to walk.
- In a small space you can put colorful stones. In a large place colored or white stones would be lovely.
- A lamp or candle holder can hang on a fence or if not put it onto the table.

- A water feature of some sort is recommended, but a fish pond is the best.
- A solar lamp.
- Ornaments of frogs or other animals.
- Dishes for food and drink.
- Elemental items such as salt or sand (Earth), feathers and incense (Air), water (Water), candles (Fire).
- Wind chimes.
- Children's windmills and other ornaments you can just press into the soil.
- Miniature furniture as used in doll houses.
- You can purchase both faery ornaments and a faery door from the internet (no iron as this repels faeries and their magic). The faery door is more of a welcoming feature and the faeries will know it is for them and see it as the entrance to their own space.
- If you do not have cats (these are not faery or bird friendly though many of us have them) then leave out bird feeders close to the faery space. If you do have cats then try to keep them in at dawn and dusk.
- A bird house can be utilized for the faeries to use or make a faery shelter.
- If you do not have an herb garden but have one planned, then plant it close to your faery garden as faeries love herbs, otherwise add some herbs to your planting.
- Ditto for a fruit and vegetable garden.

How to Care for Your Garden Faeries

- Occasionally light the candles and incense.
- Leave gemstones and offerings.
- Leave food such as honey, small cakes, wine, mead, milk, butter and cream.
- Water your plants and keep the garden weeded and trim.
- Sprinkle glitter over your faery garden from time to time, particularly in the winter when there are not so many pretty flowers or foliage.
- Feed the birds.
- Look after your *entire* garden.
- Do not use pesticides, so find some other way to control pests. You would not want to *control* your faeries in the same way you do pests!

Tips for Planting

All trees are good, but oak, ash and hawthorn are favorites. Hazel and apple are also favorite faery trees. Otherwise choose one

from the *The Faery Caille, Oracle of Wands*, in Chapter 7, after reading about each one.

My suggestions for flowers and plants are blackberry, bluebell, buttercup, calendula (marigold), carnation, clover, cowslip, daffodil, daisy, devil's-bit scabious, dogwood, fern, flax, forget-me-not, foxglove (in County Clare, Ireland, the foxglove is the faeries thimble), heather, honeysuckle, impatiens (Busy Lizzie), lavender, lilac, lobelia, orchid, pansy, peony, periwinkle, primrose, red campion, roses (miniature faery), snap dragon, St. John's wort, thistle, thyme, tulip, valerian, verbena, violet, wood sorrel, and any wildflower.

Always check if you have small children which flowers are safe to plant as many are poisonous such as the foxglove (digitalis).

Faery Window Box or Pot

You can buy a window box to keep on a sunny windowsill, inside or outside, or a saucer shaped or wide-topped pot, and put it on a table close to a sunny window. Many of the faery plants and flowers are not suitable for indoors. If you are planning for indoors, I would suggest using some faery plants along with other plants that faeries might like either for color or fragrance such as impatiens (Busy Lizzie), hyacinth

(December-January and early spring), narcissus or daffodil (early spring), snowdrop (early spring), tulip (spring), crocus (spring), orchid, thyme, verbena, heather, Boston fern, ivy, gardenia (for perfume), begonia, geranium, campanula, miniature rose, peace lily, parsley, African violet,  maidenhair fern, primrose or primula, fuchsia, jasmine, heather, azalea and coleus.

Check all plants to see they like similar conditions before buying.

Add some pebbles, or large gemstones, miniature furniture, sparkly items, thin candles and glass baubles.

Harmonia's Faery Garden

My faery garden although small at the time of writing (I have since moved), had an herb garden and water feature close by. I added large rock size gemstones of Rose and White quartz and

Blue Chalcedony. A small stool was placed at the back of the patch for my offerings, with a lamp hanging on the fence above. In the corner was a solar lamp, a candle holder and frog. Small shells lay on the table, along with gemstones, pretty pebbles, a feather and an upturned flower pot with a bird bath on top.

Planting included a miniature faery rose (pink), honeysuckle, daisies, cowslip, forget-me-not, impatiens (Busy Lizzie), carnations, buttercup, a grapevine, thyme, verbena, valerian, foxglove,  bluebells, clover, pansies, snapdragons and snowdrops. Elsewhere in my garden was thyme, sage, parsley, Echinacea, lavender, basil, mint, peppermint, rosemary, Melissa, nasturtiums, mixed flowers to attract butterflies, roses, geranium, more pansies, violet, petunias, blackberry, strawberry, daffodil, hyacinth, gardenia, poppy, holly, lily of the valley, lily, campanula, cranesbill, marigold (calendula), periwinkle, wisteria and fuchsia.

Visualization Exercise 2, *Through the Portal*

This exercise was inspired by the wonderful writings of Pete Jennings and Pete Sawyer in their book *Pathworking*.

Follow the preparations as for exercise one. Settle down and relax.

You are in a small grassy clearing in a forest. You notice a triad of trees. In front of you is a great ancient oak its leaves a bright fresh green, behind you is a tall ash which you are leaning against. To the side of you is the hawthorn tree in full bloom with delicate white flowers and fresh green leaves. The day is bright and sunny with a light breeze whispering in the trees.

Look at the oak in front of you, within its trunk there is a portal to the faery realms. Ask the faeries of the hawthorn tree can you have access to the portal.

Move forward to the great trunk and watch a hole slowly open from a small dot before you. When it is as wide as a doorway, step through. Do not be afraid of the dark.

You are suddenly carried along almost levitating towards a light at the other end. Soon you are out in another part of the forest. Immediately you see the masses of bluebells growing everywhere in carpets and pathways of lavender-blue. Look around you and you will see the sudden movements behind the trees. The faeries are here for sure but too shy to show themselves. To your right is a small but beautiful rowan tree. It has shed some leaved twigs at its base. Pick one up and attach it to you.

There is a movement in the trees and a flash of white. A great white beautiful animal with a twisted horn in the center of its forehead steps onto the path. The unicorn has come to take you through the forest.

There is a tree stump close to it. Go to the stump and use it to climb onto the back of the unicorn. Grip hold of its flowing mane as it will prevent you from falling.

The unicorn carries you onwards through the forest. Lean forward and touch its horn. It will give you the power to see the faery folk.

Now look around and you will see the folk of the forest. A dryad appears and disappears behind a tree. Small elf-like people come out from the undergrowth to watch you. You wave a friendly greeting.

You see a sylph floating through the air in front of you, she turns and looks back and then carries on forward. The unicorn comes to a halt near to a cave. You look into it and see three wrinkled old women. These are the three faery queens in their crone guise. Slide from the back of the unicorn onto the ground and enter the cave, nothing will harm you as you have your rowan twig.

As you approach the three faery queens greet them and ask if they have a message for you. They may give you something or speak to you. If after a couple of minutes nothing is given or said ask them to show it to you in another way, perhaps when you are back in your own world, then thank them and leave the cave.

The unicorn has moved to another stump so climb once more onto its back. Now wander a while and enjoy your ride through the forest and see what else you can see.

After a certain time, the unicorn will take you back, its best not to outstay your welcome. You will soon arrive safely at the great oak, take note of what you see on the way back. Slide down off the unicorn's back and thank it for its help. The portal is still open so you can enter. Perhaps a faery will come and guide you back through. You levitate back through the tunnel and emerge in your own room (or where you started) or back in the clearing.

Do not yet open your eyes. Be aware of where you are first. Take a few deep breaths and then open your eyes. Write down what you saw or heard.

Chapter 6

Faeries Of Western Europe And Scandinavia

The Child and the Faeries

The woods are full of faeries!
The trees are all alive;
The river overflows with them,
See how they dip and dive!
What funny little fellows!
What dainty little dears!
They dance and leap,
And prance and peep,
And utter fairy cheers!
Author Unknown

As discussed earlier, faeries live in another dimension, the inner space or realm of earth, which is also known as the Otherworld or Faeryland. As a result of this it would seem they are capable of appearing anywhere. It has long been suggested that faeries come into our world through portals or gateways, and also when the veil is thin between the worlds they just pass through it, which is also my belief. Once they cross over into our world, they freely move around.

Many faeries have the power of invisibility. Stepping in and out of a portal they will only reveal themselves to certain people. They might do this deliberately or sometimes accidentally. When they or we cross a ridge, an opening, or a sort of earthly black hole even, where the two dimensions cross over and the veil is imperceptible, it is possible that we find ourselves partly in their inner realm, or they find themselves partly in the earthly realm and so are visible to us. Another reason we accidentally see them, is when they — comfortable that they are in a secluded area — do not use their powers of invisibility. Perhaps this is what happened with the two irate faery men my uncle saw in the Manx countryside. Or perhaps he briefly passed into the inner realm.

A question that could be asked here is does this mean there are places — places of mystery and magic — where you more are likely to see faeries? The answer would be yes, there are such places and these places tend to have more faery sightings than anywhere else. Other places have centuries of faery related folklore which has been recorded over the years.

The next section I hope will familiarize you with some of the faery species of which a couple of tomes would be needed to record them all. Accordingly, this is just a taste of the kinds of faeries you might like or indeed might not prefer to meet.

My sister Francesca talks of faeries as being 'cosmopolitan'. And indeed faeries exist everywhere; hopefully this section will correspond either with where you live or where your interests lie.

I have begun with the Celtic countries where faery sightings are more common along with other countries rich in faery folklore. This book is not meant to be a dictionary so only a few of the many species of faeries that exist are mentioned. Some species of faery exist in more than one country. For instance many countries have dwarfs, elves and mermaids. Apologies are sincerely given if I have not included your favorite faery, or a faery common in your own country, or indeed have not included your country at all.

Ireland

Joëlle: Ireland has lots of faeries that's where most of them live.

Tanya: Ghosts can be dead faeries. They go into a human form of a ghost.

Joëlle: My friend lives in a haunted house and her friends laugh at her for believing in them. But they do exist, they were sleeping in a vacation house that once had a fire and there were two dogs killed, and they were in the vacation house and they came back to their own home with the family. When I'm there and lock the door it opens by itself.

Joëlle: Do you remember when you were playing with your friend that time, Tanya? It was freaky.

Tanya: Yes it was getting dark. We were on a space hopper and we usually go through one gate and we decided to go through another. I looked through and saw someone and asked my friend if it was her, but she was behind me. So we chucked the hopper over, and we pinched each other to make sure we were awake. Then we went away and when we came back there was nothing there. We went away and came back and she was there again. We thought it was really freaky and she had a big mark on her face.

Joëlle: It was a ghost. Where the house is, it used to be a big field by a farm and we think she must have got killed.

Tanya: Yes, there's a big field behind Joelle's friend's house, there might even be leprechauns there.

Joëlle: Leprechauns are faeries.

Tanya: If you find a four leaf clover you can give it to the leprechauns. It's for luck.

It is true that many faeries live in Ireland and of course the frequent sightings over the centuries until the present day confirm this.

In Ireland one of the explanations of the origins of faeries or the *sidhe* folk (pronounced *shee*), is that they were once fallen angels. These fallen angels were not as guilty as the rest (who were banished to hell) as they neither hindered nor helped in the revolt of Lucifer against God, but refused to be involved. It was suggested by St Michael that they should dwell on earth instead.

Faeries are also sometimes believed to be the spirits of the dead.

Among the faeries of Ireland are the Tuatha dé Danann. The Tuatha dé Danann or the people of the goddess Danu, settled in Ireland after conquering the Fir Bolg or *Firbolg* who had conquered the Fomorians who were a race of giants. The Tuatha dé Danann were in turn conquered by the Milesians and driven underground where they became the *Daoine Sidhe* or *Aes Sidhe* or faeries.

Tara Hill

Faeries in Ireland live in mounds or raths. The Hill of Tara in County Meath is one of these raths and faery rades are said to have taken or still take place there. The usual attire of the faeries is reportedly green with red caps.

There are a variety of faeries that are exclusive to Ireland,

although naturally a number emigrated to the New World with Irish families over the centuries. I am going to discuss five of the more familiar Irish faery folk, the *Leprechaun*, the *Bean Sidhe* (banshee), the *Dullahan*, the *Púka* and the *Merrow*.

Leprechauns are indisputably the most familiar of the Irish faeries, though perhaps I should be referring to them as the *Little People* to be respectful and so as not to incur their wrath! The stereotypical leprechaun is these days depicted wearing emerald green and yet he did not always appear this way, and often wore bottle-green, blue, brown or red. He has also been reported to wear red trousers, and a red cap which was commonly seen.

The leprechaun is a swarthy dwarf-like creature and is generally an ugly little man known for his longevity. He has appeared in many sizes but more often than not is reported to be around knee height.

Leprechauns are solitary folk and popularly have a hidden crock of gold. If you catch a leprechaun you can ask him to take you to his crock of gold, but you only have to take your eyes off him for a second and you will never set eyes on him again. Leprechauns are notoriously tricky and will find it easy to distract the unwary human ensuring his crock of gold will stay forever hidden.

Leprechauns take residence in old ruins, castles, monasteries, churches, caves and barns or in self-constructed buildings close to the mounds or raths or in hedgerows or groves of trees, and almost certainly in the magical triad of oak, ash, and hawthorn.

Leprechauns are partial to potatoes, which in recent centuries was a plentiful food in Ireland except perhaps in the famine years (and may have resulted in some of the leprechauns emigrating with Irish families at that time). Leprechauns sometimes steal food and drink from tables and have been known to imbibe in a little whiskey now and then.

The most common leprechaun occupation is cobbler or shoemaker. They can also be metalworkers and have other skills similar to the dwarfs. They love music and are often themselves skilled musicians.

Like many of the little people, leprechauns are frequently sighted on the Celtic festivals of Bealtaine, Summer Solstice (or around those times), and on Samhain from twilight onwards.

In Ireland I have spoken to a few people about faeries and

without exception they all mentioned the *Bean Sidhe* or *Banshee*. Some of these people, even if they had not heard her themselves, knew of those who had heard her mourning wail or keen, for the Bean Sidhe is a woman. She has even been heard in my own village. The Bean Sidhe warns of the impending death of the person she appears to, or a relative of that person. This ghostly figure has long hair and eyes red from weeping and is reported to be hideous or beautiful, old or young. There are many tales of the Bean Sidhe in Ireland and in early tales it is said that there are twenty-five headed by a queen, living in County Clare, perhaps belonging to one clan, as each clan as its own *Banshees*. If more than one Bean Sidhe gather together to give their wailing call, then it is someone holy or eminent who is going to die. The Bean

Sidhe often washes the clothes of those foretold to die, in the river until the water runs red, but is said that she cannot cross it, and will wail from the other side. She guides the souls of the dead into the Otherworld and the door should be left open to allow the spirit to leave.

Accordingly, the Bean Sidhe is a solitary faery of air who gives warning of impending death especially to the older Irish families and often but not exclusively those whose names have the prefix *Mac* or *Ó*. Hmm, perhaps I should watch out for this for my Irish family name in Old Irish is *Ó Maol Dhomnaigh*. Accordingly, I do not wish to hear the Bean Sidhe wail unless I am an extremely old lady and happy to depart this mortal coil. I am sure many would agree with me.

The *Dullahan* is another ghostly specter far more terrifying than the Bean Sidhe. He is a headless horseman who rides a jet black, headless horse. The horse's head travels with it but is detached from its body, and its eyes are a flaming red. The Dullahan is sometimes said to carry his own head on his saddle. His whip is a human spine. Where the Dullahan stops, someone is about to die. He is sometimes seen driving a black coach which is brightly lit by many skulls containing candles, and which carries a coffin. The coach is drawn by the black horse, or six of these horses. If you espy the Dullahan, he will ride to your door and fling a bowl of blood in your face, though I cannot imagine many people wishing to chance that.

The *Púka, Pooka, Phooka/Phouka* or *Pouka* (various spellings), is described as a dark or black-featured spirit and he is commonly depicted as a wicked character who can be rather vicious towards humans. However, there is talk of him as being a brownie figure that will assist with chores if befriended, but can also be a little tricky and is very much a practical joker. The Púka is a shape-shifter and sometimes shape-shifts into the form of a horse (taking those unfortunate to run into it on terror rides) and goat, but also uses the shape of the bull, eagle, bat, and ass. As a horse he treads on and spoils the blackberries. Many places are named after the Púka.

The *Merrow* is a water faery of Ireland found in the sea. The female is similar to the mermaid with a fish tail and webbed fingers. She is blessed with beauty and has long lovely hair. She loves to tease and tempt human men and sometimes even takes a human husband. Her red hat is worn cocked and it is this her husband will keep to prevent her remembering her former life, for if she finds it and puts it back on, she will remember all and return to her previous home in the sea. Sailors prefer not to see her at all as this ensures a raging storm will soon follow.

The male Merrow is ugly compared to his female counterpart and has a red nose which must clash with his green body. In fact he is entirely green, even his hair and teeth. He has short flipper-like arms and scaly skin so it is not surprising the females of the species seem to prefer human husbands to him. Although he is not a pretty sight he is a rather an amiable fellow.

I am not sure what it was I saw one rainy morning playing joyfully in Dublin Bay, perhaps it was the tail of the Merrow.

Isle of Man

The Isle of Man (from here on is shortened to 'Man') is for me a most magical place but also one of the richest in folklore. Man is reported to have more sightings of faery folk there than in any other place in the world. Having said this, I am sure there are other countries and areas that may challenge this idea.

Man was a place close to my mother's heart as she was brought up there and it is where my uncle saw the two faery men.

For those who do not know, the Isle of Man is situated in the Irish Sea between England and Ireland but is also not far from Scotland and Wales. Man is a self-governing island with a Celtic community, which was also invaded by the Norse. The Manx have their own Gaelic language as do the Irish and Scottish people.

If you travel to Man, try to visit the fairy bridge at Ballalonna Glen near Santon in the south of the island, but remember to acknowledge the faeries as you cross over the bridge by lifting your hat, or greeting them. Many people leave messages for the faeries on the bridge, and no self-respecting taxi driver will cross over it, until everyone in his cab acknowledges the faeries to prevent bad luck.

Manannán of the Tuatha dé Danann, who is Lord of the Sea, is said to be the islands first ruler and is the guardian of the gateway to the Otherworld.

Imagine walking along one of Man's pretty country roads alone on any day but particularly on Midsummer Day. Every whisper of the leaves, every movement of breeze through the grass, every butterfly flitting from wildflower to wildflower in the hedgerows, will cause you to look around furtively, as every corner of the island is a haven for the *Little People* who have been respected and accepted there for century upon century.

Below I have listed a few of the better known Manx faeries or again I should say *Little People* or *Ferrishyn*, and they are the *Fenodyree, Buggane, Lhiannan-Shee* and the *Glashtyn*. Ferrishyn is the collective name of the trooping faeries of Man. They love to ride horses and have accompanying hounds. Faery dogs are generally reported to be white with red eyes, and some black with red eyes depending on the area where they are seen. The Manx horse riders have been sighted wearing the traditional faery color of green coats and red caps.

The *Fenodyree, Fenoderee,* or *Phynnodderee* (various spellings), is essentially the Manx brownie. The Fenodyree is a solitary faery and probably did once belong to the Ferrishyn. He is a large hairy creature, who has great strength and can be a house or farm faery helping with household and agricultural tasks. Be careful how you thank the Fenodyree as he is easily offended if thanks are too profuse and he is also not happy with offerings of clothing.

The *Buggane* is not such a handsome creature either, and is described as a shape-shifting goblin able to grow to great size. As with many species of goblin he is a malevolent creature. Burning rowan wood is a protection again the Buggane who causes all sorts of mischief on land and sea.

The Buggane has also been described as an ogre type figure similar to the *Boggart* covered with black hair and with a big head and body, and long sharp teeth and nails. Whichever version you meet, he is best avoided.

The *Lhiannan-Shee* is another faery of which to be wary as she is sometimes viewed as a faery of the water. She is said to haunt springs and wells and has those qualities of the water faery in that she has the power to entice men though not in general but one particular man. If a man is entranced by her, he will be

forever in her power, never loving anyone else, and will often be driven to madness. She is possibly also a faery of the air as she appears to be a rather ethereal spirit.

A Lhiannan-Shee spirit has a connection to the fairy goblet of Ballafletcher. The crystal goblet or cup was no ordinary goblet but larger than the normal bell-shaped tumbler, and to break it would cause the family to be haunted by the Lhiannan-Shee spirit. As it was very fragile it was only used at Christmas when the Lord of the Manor would toast the spirit. He arranged for it to be kept in a strong oaken box edged with silver. The goblet was passed from person to person with the warning not to break it if they wished to preserve peace and ensure abundance. If ever anyone was unlucky enough to break it, they would suffer a terrible haunting. Last heard of, the Fairy Goblet or Cup of Ballafletcher is still preserved in the Manx Museum in Douglas.

Accordingly, in this way, the Lhiannan-Shee can also be a guardian spirit of peace albeit under certain conditions.

The *Glashtyn, Glastyn or Glashtin,* has several descriptions and has been described as a kelpie, brownie, goblin, colt, water bull, half-cow half-horse, and a water horse. However, the sprite certainly does, according to some tales, take the shape of a horse rather like the Scottish kelpie and has similar features (see below). Whatever he is or is not he is certainly not a good character to have around.

Scotland

Scotland is another Celtic country with a wealth of folklore, which is not surprising as belief in the faeries lingers on, particularly in the Highlands and Islands. A belief similar to that in Ireland is that the faeries or 'Good People' originate from the fallen angels.

The faeries of Scotland are comparable to those in the other Celtic countries, and help with chores and tasks, can be kind or malevolent, and in the past were known to steal children. They live in houses or the countryside, and the color green for clothing is favored. The faery realm in old Scots ballads is called *Elphame* or *Elfame*. This is not unlike *Alfheim* of Norse mythology.

The Seelie Court faeries — already touched upon — are the blessed faeries. The Seelie faeries are good indeed and in past times would give food gifts to the poor. They reward goodness of heart, but may teach a lesson to those whose wants exceed what is fair or necessary.

The Unseelie Court faeries are quite the opposite and not benevolent towards humankind at all. They often fly through the air and will attack travelers occasionally taking them with them on a ride of terror. Blows rain down upon the miserable victim who are sorely abused and knocked about.

The Scottish faeries I am going to discuss below are the *Kelpie*, *Gille Dubh*, *Brownie*, *Selkie*, *Bean-Nighe*, and the *Glaistig*.

The *Kelpie* is a well-known Scottish creature of the water, who resides in deep pools and rivers. He regularly appears as a water-horse and is a vicious creature and best avoided. As a shape-shifter he sometimes takes the form of a rather tatty individual and will jump on the back of unwary travelers riding in the night crushing and scaring them. But he will also drag the traveler into the water to their death. The Kelpie does have one redeeming feature in that he has been known to be called upon to assist the human. In one tale he was summoned to work by the local laird but was thoroughly disrespected and worked to exhaustion. Before disappearing into the water the Kelpie left the laird a curse that none of his family would thrive as long as the Kelpie was still alive. Accordingly this indicates that even if some are (and that is not certain), not all faeries are immortal if the Kelpie will, in time, die.

The *Gille Dubh* or *Ghillie Dhu* is a Scottish tree dweller. He prefers to occupy the birch tree or birch thickets. Rather strange in looks, he is reported to have wild black hair and clothes woven of leaves and moss. He is a private creature, and although he avoids contact with others, he is known to be compassionate, especially towards children. Tales tell of the Gille Dubh who helped a young Mackenzie girl, and having looked after her for the night escorted her home. In later years another Mackenzie, Sir Hector of Gairloch, gathered together five lairds to hunt the Gille Dubh as

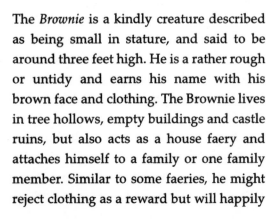

a trophy but to no avail as you will be glad to know, I am sure.

The *Brownie* is a kindly creature described as being small in stature, and said to be around three feet high. He is a rather rough or untidy and earns his name with his brown face and clothing. The Brownie lives in tree hollows, empty buildings and castle ruins, but also acts as a house faery and attaches himself to a family or one family member. Similar to some faeries, he might reject clothing as a reward but will happily accept a bowl of cream and a piece of honeycomb. Like many of the faeries he is only tricky when he sees misdemeanors committed and then will mildly punish the offending person.

The *Selkie* or *Silkie* is a creature who dwells beneath the sea and is frequently seen on Orkney or Shetland. Selkies take the form of a seal at sea but when they come onto land they take a human form. They are beautiful creatures, who like many water faeries, will marry into the human species. The male will pursue a female human but will not stay with her. The female likewise is attracted to the human male and he is attracted to her. However, if either sex has the seal skin stolen they cannot return to the sea and are destined to forever stay in the human world.

The *Bean-Nighe* bears much similarity to the Irish *Bean-Sidhe* but is a water spirit. She is a messenger from the Otherworld who comes to warn of impending death. As 'Washer at the Ford' she sits at the ford or stream and washes the blood from the funeral clothes of those who are about to pass over, particularly those in battle. Like the Bean-Sidhe she wears green but is portrayed as an old woman with long drooping breasts, buck teeth (or one buck tooth), and webbed feet. If the person whose death she is forewarning manages to suckle from one of her breasts, they will be spared...Yuk!

The *Glaistig* is a satyr-like creature and is sometimes portrayed as half-woman, half-goat. The Glaistig does show similarities to the *Bean-Nighe* in that she is a water spirit, and seldom seen anywhere than beside streams. Like her counterparts she also dresses in green. Unlike the Bean-Nighe she is attractive or even beautiful and although more often see as a benevolent faery can also appear as malevolent. However, in the guise as the 'Green Glaistig' she is the former. She mourns both chronic illness and death, especially if she is familiar with the family. Known to help people by protecting them and their cattle, the Glaistig is a faery guardian. However, if you are rude or disrespectful to her she will withdraw her kindness.

Wales

Welsh mythology is powerful and perhaps it is the Mabinogion along with Arthurian legend that continually holds the interest of many, including me. If you want to discover the faery folk, Wales is one of the most beautiful places on earth to find them. Welsh scenery is stunning, extremely pretty, and often wild. It has mountains, sea, lakes, rivers, and sacred wells. Wales is a mystical place and no one needs to persuade me of it.

Once, when I was a student, a few of us with our favorite tutor went to look for a hidden but mystical holy well on the Lleyn Peninsula at midnight. After some trouble we found it and we sat down on the various levels of stone surrounding the large pool of water in the ground. We waited in charged silence almost expecting something to rise out of the water. The eerie atmosphere was powerful and it was one of the most mystical experiences any of us ever had.

On that same residential trip, I saw something strange on the beach at dusk one evening. A few of us had gone to the beach and had placed ourselves on stones a little way apart from each other and we meditated in silence lulled by the hypnotic motion of the waves. At one point I glanced to the side and saw that someone had silently joined us and was sitting some little way away from me. I thought it was a small lady, who was also one of the students, but seconds later when I looked again there was no one there except the flat stone, and the beach was empty save those of us who arrived together. Whether it was a faery or spirit I saw I will never know, but for sure Wales has its fair share of both.

There are many other wonderful places where faeries appear in Wales. North to mid-Wales is particularly magical and rich in faery lore, as well as having beautiful and majestic scenery.

However, there is hardly anywhere in Wales where you will not find one faery or another.

The faeries of Wales I will discuss are the *Tylwyth Teg*, the *Ellyllon, Ellylldan, Pwca, Coblynau, Gwyllion*, the *Gwragedd Annwn* and the *Bwbach*.

The chief race of faeries in Wales is the *Tylwyth Teg*. The Tylwyth Teg faeries are the fair folk who love all the things for which faeries are famous, such as music, dancing in the moonlight, or the granting of wishes. They can also be angered by those who are disrespectful to them. Stealing children or swapping them for changelings and marrying into the human race is common among them. Unlike some faery races, the Tylwyth Teg appear to be beautiful and rather elegant, and although their clothing can vary in color, green is again the most favored.

The *Ellyllon* are pretty, elf-like faeries, and some folklorists agree that the foxglove (digitalis) is connected with them. Again they have the attributes of many of their good faery counterparts and are helpful and generous to those who respect them.

Wales also has a fair share of malevolent faeries and the *Ellylldan* are among these. They are a mischievous faery similar to the *Will-o'-the-Wisp*, and they lead unwary travelers into bogs.

The *Pwca* is said to be another name for the Ellylldan and is also similar to the *Púka* of Ireland. Cwm Pwca, or Puck Valley, is a romantic glen of the Clydach Gorge in Breconshire which was possibly the location for *A Midsummer's Night Dream* in which Puck himself became so renowned. Before being industrialized the valley was said to have been a beautiful place. The Pwca can lead unwary folk into danger and derives much fun from it.

The *Coblynau* are similar to the *Knockers* of Cornwall in that they are mine faeries or goblins. They are reported to be about knee high and rather ugly though are friendly folk. Like the knockers they make a knocking noise to indicate the location of the ore, and although they look busy with their miner's gear they actually do no work themselves. They throw stones if provoked but do not hurt anyone.

My own theory for mine workers who look busy hammering away but seeming to achieve nothing is rather like when we leave crystals in trees only to find them still there later as only the spirit of the crystal is taken. With the mine-working goblins they are actually achieving something as they work, not for the human folk but for themselves and their yield is taken back to the Otherworld.

The *Gwyllion*, as I mentioned earlier, is a faery to be avoided at all costs. This malicious female faery of the mountains will lead the traveler astray. She will frequently appear as an old lady. The Gwyllion can be defeated by iron. Faeries in general dislike iron and it is said to repel magic. So if you want to attract faeries do not put iron ornaments on your faery table.

The *Gwragedd Annwn*, are faeries of the Welsh lakes and rivers, especially those that are high up in the mountainous regions. They are not malicious at all and are both friendly and beautiful. They make their homes in faery palaces or castles. As with many water faeries, humans are attracted to them, but unlike some water faeries, the human will go willingly to them and as they do not entice.

There are tales of a Lady of the Lake in which a human farm worker or ploughman catches her and she becomes his bride. As with many folk or faery tales there are variations of this. The Lady of the Lake comes willingly enough, but is lost when the ploughman strikes her three unwarranted blows. These blows seem to be hardly blows at all but more of a heavy hand on the shoulder. However, the faery bride leaves him and her sons and returns to the lake from whence she came along with the dowry of stock, including goats, cattle and horses. Her sons would walk by the lake in the hope of seeing her, until one day she appeared to her eldest son and told him he should become learned in medicines and herbs, and in learning this skill he and his family should use it for the benefit of humankind. And this he did, and he and his brothers returned to the lake and gradually learned from their mother the great skills of herbal medicine. The eldest son passed this knowledge onto his own sons and so it goes on.

I decided to add a little about this last faery as it is a faery of the household. The *Bwbach* (plural is *Bwbachod*), is a friendly brownie type faery, who helps in the house and dairy in exchange for a bowl of cream. He appears to favor those who are partial to a sup of strong ale. However, he does tend to tease or annoy those who abstain from this particular pleasure. Perhaps they are a little too pious for his liking.

Cornwall

The wild and breathtaking scenery of beautiful Cornwall with its mild climate is the next area I wish to include, as it is a county in England that is particularly rich in faery folk. Cornwall deserves its own mention as much as the Isle of Man and other places of the British Isles. The legends of Arthur and his magical castle at Tintagel, the famous piskies, giants, witches and wizards, can all be found in Cornwall along with ancient sites and stone circles.

The faeries in general are called the small people, but I am going to look at four types of Cornish faeries, the *Piskies*, the *Spriggans*, the *Knockers* and the *Browneys*. I recommend Dozmary Pool on Bodmin Moor as a place to visit as it is reported to be the haunt of the *Lady of the Lake* of Arthurian legend and also the lake where Sir Bedivere threw Excalibur after the mortal wounding of King Arthur.

You cannot visit Cornwall without coming across the *Piskies*, who are much older and have a more wizened appearance than their West Country piskey or piskie neighbors of Devon and Somerset. Deeply set in their wrinkled faces their eyes are bright and intelligent and hold a glint of mischief. Their clothing as with many faeries can differ from story to story. They can be smartly dressed in browns, or not so smartly dressed in tattered greens. Piskies are helpful and generous and like to be repaid with a smart suit of clothes, which might account for the fact that sometimes they are smart and other times are rather ragged.

The *Spriggans* as I have mentioned before are trooping faeries. They are guardians of treasure and can be found in those places where treasure is likely to be, such as castles, caves, and old ruins. The Spriggans are not the prettiest of creatures and are in fact rather ugly. They are not the pleasantest either and have been known to steal children exchanging them for their own ugly changeling brats. They cause mischief and bring ill luck and cause bad weather to ruin crops and are certainly best avoided.

The *Knockers* or *Buccas* are the mining sprites and if you have the read the above on the *Coblynau* Welsh faery, there are great similarities. The Knockers knock when they find the rich ore of the mines. They mine for themselves as do the Coblynau and are ugly creatures. Respect the Knockers if you want to continue with the good luck that they can bring, as they can just as easily give you trouble if you treat them badly. Knockers like to have gifts of food.

The *Browneys* are guardians of bees. They can be called upon to help with the task of rounding up swarming bees and to help them settle again. In times of old (and who knows perhaps this is still done) the Cornish housewife would go out and bang on a tin and call out to the Browney to come to her assistance.

England

England falls in the center of these Celtic areas and countries and has its own wealth of faeries from the north to south and from east to west. Many faeries can be found in the lovely countryside. Each county has its own wealth of folklore and its own particular faery (or faeries) and creatures. Frequent sightings suggest that many an English garden has faeries, particularly the winged flower faery.

Some of the most magical places to discover faeries can be found in England so take your pick among bluebell woods in spring, beautiful parks and stately home gardens, little hamlets and villages, forests, spectacular mountainous areas, breathtaking hills and dales, lakes and rivers, the untamed coastal areas, magical caves, and wild heath and moorland.

I have had my own magical experiences in Wiltshire as I relate elsewhere in this book, but there are other particular English places where I have had similar experiences, and these include Derbyshire, Cheshire, Somerset and Lancashire.

I have chosen to introduce a mixture of faeries from north and south, *The Grant, Robin Goodfellow*, the *Will-o'-the-Wisp, Goblin/Hobgoblin* (they deserved a mention somewhere), the *Boggart, Pixie, Churnmilk Peg* and *Melch Dick*.

The *Grant* is a young foal that runs through English villages on his hind legs to whinny a warning. In his flight through the village streets he causes much commotion as it upsets the dogs. When the people hear him they are can be on the lookout for impending disasters.

Robin Goodfellow is a hobgoblin who is also known as *Puck*. When you think of the name *Robin Goodfellow* it conjures up an agreeable 'Robin Hood of the Forest' character, while *Puck* conjures up the cheeky chappy of Shakespeare always looking for mischief. Robin Goodfellow is however, indeed sometimes equated with Robin Hood. He is also occasionally portrayed as a half-man, half-goat satyr, who is associated with Pan of the forest. More often he is depicted as a hairy character and less often as a boyish one. One of the things that mischievous and malevolent faeries like to do is to confuse night travelers causing them to be lost and Robin Goodfellow is no exception. As a shape-shifter he has been known to be able to turn himself into a horse or foal and other animals. He has counterparts in the Irish *Púka* and Welsh *Pwca*.

The *Will-o'-the-Wisp* is a small light that is seen at night often over boggy ground. It flickers in the half-light or mist.

The Will-o'-the-Wisp is sometimes portrayed as another forest character occasionally associated with Puck and Pwca, and described as a small sprite. He is generally mischievous and will cause you to lose your way as do many faeries of this kind.

The *Goblin* and *Hobgoblin* are mentioned several times in this book. The goblin is the more sinister of the two while the hobgoblin is the 'Robin Goodfellow' type of faery. The *Goblin* is small, mean and nasty. He is malevolent and can cause great harm. The goblin is the bad guy of many fantasy and faery stories. He is smelly, scruffy, and dirty, with ragged clothing and has nasty yellow or green teeth and bad breath. He is generally grotesque in appearance. The *Hobgoblin* is a little less ugly and smelly and has been known to assist folk even though he can cause mischief.

The *Boggart* is a faery of Yorkshire. He is a spirit that is invisible and who executes a poltergeist type of activity. He torments families, including the children of the family and it is not easy to rid your household of him. If he attaches himself to you, moving to another home will not work as he will move with you. Some other method to rid your home of this unwelcome visitor, if you cannot befriend him, will be necessary.

The *Pixie* as opposed to the Piskie of neighboring Cornwall (also called the Piskie or another spelling of this) favors Devon and Somerset though he is seen in other English counties such as Dorset and Hampshire. He is not as wizened as his Cornish neighbor or relative, the Piskie. Pixies are generous and helpful but are not so friendly to those who anger or disrespect them, and regularly play the usual tricks of causing travelers to lose their way. They love flowers, especially tulips, have pointy ears and red hair, often wear green, and can also shape-shift to human size.

Churnmilk Peg is a dryad of North Yorkshire. She is sighted wearing medieval peasant clothing and is a guardian of all nut trees found in England. Her counterpart is Melch Dick. Children cannot steal the nuts or Churnmilk Peg will catch them. She is a lazy creature as is her associate; however, they cannot abide laziness in others. Perhaps they are lazy because they are old and wizened and have arthritis and general aches and pains so we should perhaps count their laziness as being forced upon them.

Melch Dick is the male equivalent of Churnmilk Peg and also guards the nut trees and thickets of the West Riding of Yorkshire from children. These two dryads will pinch you and give you the most horrible stomach ache should you venture to steal the nuts from the trees.

Brittany
Brittany (North-West France) is a Celtic land of wild coastline, green fields and woodland. Brittany is a peninsula and has an abundance of megalithic monuments. Dolmens and menhirs are scattered throughout the region. The Celtic Breton language is still spoken by some of the people mostly in the western areas.

The magical forest of Broceliande in eastern Brittany is a 'must see' place to visit and here lie the legends of Arthur, Merlin and Vivien. The tree in which Merlin was imprisoned by the Vivien (or the Lady of the Lake), is in this forest, and you will also discover the magical spring or fountain of Baranton or Bérenton. The water of the fountain can cause storms, and the sprinkling of it onto a nearby magical stone can cause the person who pours it to become clairvoyant.

The faeries, *fée* or *fées* of Brittany mentioned here are the *Korrigan*, the *Morgan*, the *Ankou* and *Vivien*.

The *Korrigan* or *Corrigan* faeries are small red-eyed dwarf-sized women who can shape-shift. They have much beauty and have long golden hair by night or twilight, but are old and wrinkled by day. They love to dance in the moonlight especially at the time of the Full Moon and wear white woolen or course linen robes. The Korrigans are mainly seen at twilight or perhaps in the night. Perhaps this is not surprising as like anyone they would want to be seen in their best light, especially as they are renowned for luring handsome young men into their clutches, to sexually unite with them to ensure their species is continued. The poor young men die with love for these creatures. The best way to avoid the Korrigan is by staying away from the Breton dolmens at twilight and darkness, and anytime the veil between words is thinner. Children should be protected as the Korrigan are child thieves.

The *Morgan* or *Morgen* is a water faery who lives in a bejeweled palace beneath the sea. Preferring to sleep by day she emerges onto the rocks in the moonlight to comb her long golden locks. She entices the sailor as she sings her plaintive melody, but just as she gets him in her clasp he is doomed to die, and so she goes on desperately searching for a human man to love her.

The *Ankou* is the Breton equivalent of the sinister character *Death* or perhaps the *Dullahan* or *Bean Sidhe* and collects the souls of the dead by knocking on the door for them. He transports them to the Otherworld along certain pathways. He visits all Breton families in this way not just choosing particular ones.

Vivien deserves a mention here as she is said to be the mysterious faery 'The Lady of the Lake' of Arthurian legend. Brittany has its own tales of King Arthur along with Wales, Cornwall and other southern counties of England.

There are many versions of this legend, but it seems that disguised as a youth Merlin was wandering through the forest of Broceliande when he came across a fountain and sat down to rest. Vivien, a beautiful young woman, who was daughter of the Lord of the Manor of Broceliande, came to the fountain. Her father was loved by the *Fée* who promised him that his daughter in turn would be loved by the wisest man in the world. The *Fée* added that all her wishes would be granted by this wise man, and sinisterly, that he would never be able to force her to comply with his own.

As Merlin rose to leave the area, he exchanged glances with the lovely Vivien. She asked him who he was and he told her he was a student learning the arts of magic. He demonstrated some of his magical powers. Vivien expressed a wish to also practice magic, and Merlin promised to teach her in time. He arranged to meet her again after the passing of one full year.

After that year, Merlin met Vivien once more and fell totally under her power as his love for her was strong. She asked for the secrets of magic for a spell to cause her parents to sleep, so she could stay with Merlin without them knowing. Not being able to resist her, Merlin agreed. After Vivien performed the magic they were then able to spend many joyful days together. It was not the youth aspect of him that Merlin presented to her that Vivien was beguiling, as she knew full well this was Merlin the wisest of men. Vivien asked for one further spell, which Merlin was unable to resist. She wanted him to be her slave of love, forever bound to her, and he granted this. In this Breton tale, Merlin happily settled down to stay in the enchanted forest with his love Vivien, never to return to the world of mortals again.

Germany

Germany has a rich culture of folklore and who can forget the tales of the Brothers Grimm as they are famous all over the world. German mythology is similar to that of Scandinavia. The German god *Wotan*, along with the Anglo-Saxon *Woden* and Dutch *Wodan*, is Odin in the Norse Pantheon. *Dwarfs* are prevalent as in Norse mythology and folklore and even though I have mentioned them in that section, I think they deserve a short mention here too. *Nixies* also appear in both cultures and I have included *Kobolds*, *Lorelei* and *Frau Holda* in my discussion.

Dwarfs in German folklore are more often than not friendly (as in Snow White) and live in the mountains, hills, caves and under-ground. They possess the power of magic and can become invisible. Dwarfs are generally skilled in crafts particularly metalwork and can be generous if they wish, and German Dwarfs are no exception.

The epic poem *The Nibelungenlied* or *Lay of the Nibelung*, was passed down from the oral tradition before it was written down rather like the Eddas in the Middle Ages. Several versions exist of this, but one tale tells of a Dwarf called Alberich who was the guardian of a hoard of treasure and who also had the power of invisibility. *Wagner* later used the myth when he composed his opera, *Des Ring des Nibelungen*. *Nibelung* is thought to mean *Dwarf*. From this epic poem we gain much information about Dwarfs and the services they perform and the way in which they live.

Other sources describe Dwarfs as wearing mist-caps to render them invisible so they can go about unnoticed. However, if the mist-cap is knocked from their little heads they can be seen quite clearly.

Disrespect for the *little folk* caused them to disappear in many areas of Germany and they are now little seen.

Nixies or *Nixes* live in the lakes and rivers of Germany and there are male and female of this species. The men wear green hats and have green teeth, and the women like to sit on the rocks or river bank in the same way as other water women, combing their long beautiful, golden locks. The women fall in love with human men and have been known to drag them down under the water. Their melodious songs entrance these men, putting them under a spell which in time drives them to madness. Other Nixies leave the water to shop among human folk in the markets.

Human midwives have occasionally been called upon by the water men to help in the labor of their wives and to safely deliver the baby. However there is some danger attached to this duty and nothing in the Nixie home must be touched and no more payment then usual taken.

The *Lorelei* or *Loreley* is a water faery who sits on the rocks of the Rhine again combing her long hair. Like a siren she lures sailors to their deaths by singing her entrancing song.

There is more than one type of *Kobold*. One is a brownie-like house faery who assists in all household duties. He is an amiable fellow and if well looked after, will stay in the household and behave perfectly. Treat him badly or neglect him however, then the family should watch out as he can be dangerous. Another type of Kobold haunts mines or other underground places.

Frau Holda, Holle, or *Huldra* (Scandinavia), is the faery patron of spinning and weaving. She is the equivalent of the good Faery Godmother. She often appears during the twelve days of Christmas and rewards hard work and industry. As many faery queens do, she can appear in two forms, one an old woman with crooked teeth and nose, and the other a beautiful young woman all dressed in white (Scandinavia).

Another version of the frau appears in a faery tale of the Brothers Grimm in which a young girl sitting by a well pricks her finger and drops her spindle into the water. With great consternation at the loss of the spindle she jumps into the well and finds herself in the home of Frau Holda. Her industrious spinning earns her a reward and she is sent back to her mother covered with gold. Her mother sends her other daughter to copy her sister's actions in the hope of more gold. However, the sister is too lazy and is covered with pitch as her reward.

The Netherlands

Although a small country the Netherlands also has faeries, but perhaps the most well-known are the Kabouter, and the Witte Wieven. Although the Netherlands is largely flat it does have forests and rivers in which the little folk can happily live.

Children here love faeries as much as those in other countries. While walking with my husband along a path through a wood, we saw a grandfather and two small children. The grandfather was collecting some wood and the children who were about four or five years old were discussing elves and how they like to sit on toadstools among the trees.

The *Kabouter* is similar to the German Kobold. The men are commonly depicted as gnome-like with long beards and pointed red hats with blue jackets. The women wear peasant dress. They can be as small as a few inches in height. Generally, they make their homes underground often building their houses in the roots of trees. As with most gnomes and dwarves the Kabouters do have a variety of skills and work in crafts which include weaving, basket making and carpentry, but also in husbandry and healing and often become house faeries. They also said to speak their own language and write in rune script. Kabouters are friendly but shy, and perhaps the best place to find them is in the forest.

The Witte Wieven (*Witte Vrouwen* or *Witte Juffers*), are the spirits of wise women or priestesses, and haunt the forest, lakes, swamps, hills and megaliths. They also exist in Belgium, France and Germany. Although *witte* translates as *white* in modern Dutch it is said to mean 'wise' or 'wit' in *Low Saxon*. These wise women are healers, have knowledge of herbs and are prophets. As with many faeries they were given elf-like, or *alven*, status as they remained on earth as spirits after death. Offerings are given to them is return for help. In older Christian times they were reduced to satanic witch-like creatures. As a result they have good and bad press. They can help you or be tricky and may exchange your child for a sickly changeling.

Scandinavia

Scandinavia has a wealth of faeries not least *Elves, Dwarfs, Giants,* and *Trolls.*

I cover a little more about their worlds and Yggdrasil the World Tree further below in The Faery Caille in Chapter 7, and also in my book *The Spiritual Runes.* But here is a brief introduction. No one knows for sure exactly which realms are included in the nine realms of Yggdrasil, the World Tree that makes up the Norse Cosmology, or where exactly they are situated, so this is from my own research. You will find in the accounts of others that realms may vary slightly and be positioned differently. *Alfheim* is the realm of the *Light Elves* and is situated in the higher realms of Yggdrasil along with *Asgard* (the realm of the Aesir gods) and *Vanaheim* (the realm of the Vanir gods).

The realm of the dark elves (who are interchangeable with dwarfs) is *Svartalfheim* and is situated in the earthly realms along with *Midgard,* the realm of humankind and *Jotunheim,* the realm of the Jotuns or frost giants.

The remaining three realms are in the lower regions or underworld and are *Muspelheim,* the realm of the fire giants, *Niflheim,* a frozen wasteland, and *Hel* or *Helheim,* which is the realm of the dead.

Elves appear in all Teutonic mythology. As with all faeries, elves can be helpful or malicious. The *Light Elves* are fairer than humans, and are most beautiful to look upon, and just like others faeries of their kind, they love to dance, especially in the moonlight. Like us they have societies and kings and queens.

Alfheim lies in the higher realms of Yggdrasil and these realms are heavenly places. Alfheim is a wonderful land of nature, beauty and magic and is ruled by Frey the god of fertility, sun and rain, and who is the patron of the bountiful harvest. According to legend, Alfheim was given to Frey as a tooth-gift.

The palace of Frey can be found there. As occupants of Alfheim, the Light Elves are the benevolent creatures that help humans with general work unless treated unfairly, or the person becomes greedy. At this point the work is undone or they disappear.

The *Dark Elves* are as dark as pitch and as ugly as sin. They are hairy individuals with hump backs and crooked noses. They are also associated with stealing human children and substituting them for changelings. In Norse mythology they also appear as the *Dwarfs*. Dark places underground are favored by them and their realm is Svartalfheim which is situated below Midgard the realm of humankind.

Dwarfs in the past were described in a negative way as malignant faeries. As they have been known to be benevolent too, this is rather an unfair view. The Dwarfs are a race of workers of skilled craftsmen, commonly goldsmiths and black-smiths. Four Dwarfs made the beautiful necklace of

Brisingamen, which Freyja wanted to buy, but they would only agree to sell if she would sleep one night with each of them, which she did. Dwarf women do not appear to exist so it is thought they took women from other faery species perhaps even human women.

Dwarfs also made other special items for the gods, including Sif's beautiful golden hair, and *Mjollnir*, Thor's hammer, *Skidbladnir*, Frey's ship, and *Gungnir* and *Draupnir*, Odin's spear and ring.

The Dwarf Dvalin (or Dvalinn) was said to have passed on the knowledge of runic writing to the Dwarfs and another called Dain (or Dainn), to the Elves.

Like elves, *Giants* can be helpful or malicious. They appear throughout mythology and play a large part in Ragnarok, the Norse Day of Judgment.

The *Frost Giants* or Jotuns, reside in Jotunheim on the middle levels of Yggdrasil. The trolls who appear in later myths and legends come from these. The first giant Ymir, appears in the Norse creation myth.

The *Fire Giants* reside in Muspelheim in the lower realms. They are involved with the devastation of Yggdrasil at Ragnarok when many of the gods will die. As they ride over Bifrost the Rainbow Bridge to the higher realms, it collapses, while Midgard is destroyed on the way.

Giants played a huge part in the life of the god Frey. He fell in love with one giant which led to his death by another. It began with Frey falling in love with the giantess Gerd, daughter of Gymir the frost giant. After her initial rejection, his servant Skirnir won her round using the magical runes. Frey gave up his magical sword which was forged by the dwarfs, to the servant as a reward. At Ragnarok he is unable to properly defend himself and he is killed by the fire giant Surt.

The *Trolls* have two views of them. One is that of a large, dark creature who is extremely ugly and malevolent. The other is less ugly and is inclined to be friendly.

It appears the Trolls originated from the earlier giants and are a later addition to Scandinavian mythology. Throughout Scandinavia, there are differences between the Trolls appearances, behavior, size and names.

Trolls live underground, within hills, or in caves and even in palaces. Although inclined to be thieves, the friendly Trolls are helpful to humankind and marry and have their own families. In general Trolls are shape-shifters and dislike noise, are skilled in crafts, and have the power of invisibility but dislike daylight. They have been known to abduct children and leave changelings in their place, as well as kidnapping people to enslave. Often they are guardians of treasure.

Chapter 7

The Faery Caille, *Oracle Of Wands*

The Faery Caille is my own divination system based on the twentieth-century version of the Ogham Alphabet and other divination systems, and is influenced by the elements of earth, air, fire and water. The Faery Caille is not an alphabet; it is purely a faery tree divination system. In the *Caille* however, you may find that some of the tree meanings will contain similar elements. However, I have researched each tree separately from the Ogham and so this oracle is rather subjective.

This is a form of divining that works remarkably well and I have primarily designed it to help you in connecting with and contacting the faery folk, while learning a little about trees, which are sacred to them.

Ogham

Ogham is an ancient alphabet which was used mainly in Ireland although some inscriptions have also been discovered in Britain. The original basic alphabet consisted of twenty letters and symbols.

The letter symbols of Ogham were written as simple straight lines, some lying diagonally. Additional to these twenty letters, are five more letters which were thought to have been added in mediaeval times, and which are now more often than not used in divining in more recent decades.

The letters did not all originally have tree symbols, this is said to have been interpreted incorrectly by mediaeval scholars. More modern research shows that only seven or eight of the original twenty letters are trees. Ogham was more often used in inscribing, but some myths do indicate it was perhaps used in divining too, usually in relation to the discovery of locations. However in more recent times, the tree interpretation of Ogham is most often used in divining.

One thing is certain in all this *uncertainty* surrounding Ogham is that just as with the Tarot, it works very well regardless of the original usage and interpretation. Although some writers do provide incorrect information, based on the incorrect information of others who have gone before them, some researchers miss the point when they deride the modern Ogham. All that matters to those that use it is that it works. And the various modern divination systems of Ogham do work, and I have used one of these for several years now.

The Faery Caille

The Faery Caille has 19 tree symbols. Three are the great magical triad of trees of Oak, Ash and Hawthorn, called the *Faery Portal*. The 16 others are called the *Faery Wands*. The Faery Wands are further divided into four elemental groups of four wands each, *earth* (gnomes), *air* (sylphs), *water* (undines), and the fourth *fire* (salamanders). The two additional wands are the Elementals Wand (Gnome, Sylph, and Undine), and the Salamander Wand (fire), which have a significant effect on the 19 Faery Wands as you will see. This adds up to a total of 21 wands which is a multiple of *three*, a magical number, or three times *seven*, also a magical number. The Faery Caille is made from 21 wands of wood; however, they can also be inscribed onto card.

Connection and Communication

In my book *The Spiritual Runes*, I have covered how divination systems can teach you to become in touch with hidden and often neglected aspects of your psyche. In the same way using a divination system will also help you in communicating and connecting with the faeries.

Divination increases your psychic skills because in reading the symbols you call on hidden intuitiveness to help you in interpreting. When using a divination tool, the symbols or pictures act as a catalyst for communication between your conscious and unconscious self, and/or you and a spirit power. You become part of this channel of communication. Through the divination tool you learn to see what has previously been invisible to you. The chosen tool will help to trigger something deep in your psyche and therefore it is important to look at, learn, and relate to the symbols and pictures, not to just to read the accompanying words. That way you will pick up messages psychically over and above what someone else has written as the basic meaning.

To begin with, I will explain the symbols and meaning of the wands. This will follow with an explanation of how to use the system and how to make your own set. Finally, I will demonstrate how you can use the Faery Caille to help you in your everyday life.

I have intermingled faeries with certain gods and goddesses. Some Irish deities were 'degenerated' or 'reduced' to the role of faery. However, this depends on the viewpoint you take. For me faeries are not lesser beings as such. Though perhaps not equal in power, they exist in the same realms as the gods and goddesses, and the interconnection between mythological deities and faeries such as dwarfs, elves and giants is a strong one.

You can use the *contact* suggestions for extra magical and spiritual assistance, and also if you have a negative reading.

I have included a table of one sentence 'quick' references for each wand, and a table of faeries, contact days and offerings, at the end of the chapter.

You can use the oracle of wands in more than one way. If you have a problem and you recognize it among the wands, either with the normal or negative reading, you can look at the 'contact' suggestions to see how the faeries and the power of the accompanying tree can help you.

The Oak, Ash and Hawthorn Portal

Of all the trees that grow so fair,
Old England to adorn,
Greater is none beneath the sun,
Than Oak, and Ash, and Thorn.
Sing Oak, and Ash, and Thorn, good sirs,
(All of a Midsummer morn!)
Surely we sing of no little thing,
In Oak, and Ash, and Thorn!
From *A Tree Song*, Rudyard Kipling

The triad of trees; oak, ash and hawthorn, is a magical combination and a portal to the Otherworld. The hawthorn tree protects the portal entrance or entrances of the other two trees of oak and ash.

Here, they are presented as the Faery Portal. Each one of the triad has a special meaning in the Faery Oracle. If one turns up in your reading then it means something significant in your life. It also means the faeries are there for you should you want to contact them.

The Oak Portal
Strength and Success
Element: Fire

The Oak Tree
The oak tree is perhaps the most revered tree of all and is known as the 'Father of the Woods'. It was not just the Druids and Celts

that held this tree sacred, but also the Greek, Roman and Teutonic peoples.

The Druids are thought to have worshipped the oak in groves. Mistletoe, also a sacred plant of the Druids, can occasionally be entwined in the oak's branches. The oak represents strength and endurance yet it is struck by lightning more than any other tree, most probably owing to low electrical resistance. Accordingly, it is not surprising that it is associated with the element *fire*.

In Norse mythology the oak is the tree of Thor the god of thunder, lightning and storms, and protector of humankind. Thor represents all the attributes of the oak, of strength, valiance, courage and protector against the forces of evil. Zeus was the Greek chief of gods and was also the god of an oracle established at an oak tree (although sometimes this is the beech) at Dodona in Greece.

Folklore

There is an old folk rhyme which talks of *turning your cloak* because *faery folks are in old oaks*. Turning your outer clothing such as your jacket or cloak, would protect you from the faeries, especially if you were traveling in remote areas.

The oak is the tree of the dryad, a female nymph-like nature spirit. The dryad inhabits the oak tree and blends in with it as she is shy. She usually stays within sight of her tree, and will rarely move more than three hundreds yards from it. Although when she does, she is sometimes pursued by the hot-blooded satyr, a spirit of the woods and mountains, who is half-human and half-goat and has the horns of a goat or is described as having a horse's tail. The dryad stays with the tree for life and dies with it, so can live for centuries. If the tree is destroyed by mortals then that mortal should watch out, for the faery folk may seek revenge.

The Oakmen are strange dwarf-like creatures. They are ugly like most dwarfs and act as guardians of the oak and oak groves. They are said to wear red caps and like many faery folk they are reclusive or shy, but are not harmful.

The oak appears in the mythology of many peoples, and is one of the trees which has an affinity with the goddess (also saint) Brigid. Some myths tell us she is the daughter of the Celtic faery ruler or sun god the Dagda. The Dagda, also according to certain myths, was born of *Bile* the oak tree together with the goddess *Danu* who watered it. Brigid is the patron of the fire, the forge, the hearth, craftsmanship (especially blacksmiths), poetry, childbirth and healing.

The Dagda was a huge figure in the faery world, a ruler who battles for and protects his people the Tuatha Dé Danann. He carried a magic harp made from oak which he took into battle.

The Oak King is a powerful giant figure of nature wearing oak foliage. He rules the half year from the Winter Solstice (Yule), until the Summer Solstice after defeating his twin brother the Holly King, who in turn rules from the Summer Solstice until the Winter Solstice. The Oak king is the king of light and the waxing year.

The oak can be counted among the most sacred of faery trees for contact with faery.

The Oak Portal in a Reading: The oak stands stalwart and noble. It grows tall and solid and is respected and revered by all. This giant of a tree ensures solidity and stability, particularly in family life. Someone may enter your life to provide leadership and direction. Take the advice of the wise one. Hold onto and appreciate what you have, protect your family and home to ensure future stability. Once this is achieved, you can move forward with confidence that you have a stable base on which to build. If you have already achieved this then it is time to move forward along your life pathway. You have earned that right along with the respectability you deserve.

The dryads and the oakmen offer protection in the face of adversity. Any outside influences attempting to thwart your plans, will be kept at bay. When you take the courage to move forward you might have insecurities about what the future holds. Take heart, you are protected just as the oak is, and can walk forward tall and proud.

Brigid as granddaughter of the oak offers success and prosperity for hard work. This success is not yours by right it has to be earned. This hard work can pertain to physical work of any craft, or of inspirational work such as poetry. She will also bring you protection in pregnancy or childbirth, and healing if you have been unfortunate enough to have suffered ill health.

Her father, the Dagda — as son of the oak, reinforces the oak's strength and protection in his father-like qualities, protector of his tribe, wisdom, strength in battle and strength against adversity. Any obstacles you face when the door of opportunity opens will be overcome so take courage, you have it in you.

The Oak Portal appearing in a reading denotes strength in all situations faced, along with stability, reward, prosperity, good health and protection. You are assured of these things, but remember to appreciate and protect what is yours, and take wise advice given.

The Oak Portal is opening up to you. This means that once you have ensured your security there is a whole world awaiting you.

Negative Reading: If the Oak Portal appears with the negative Salamander Wand it is barely affected, but indicates minor insecurities or delays. Use the contact information below to request strength and courage and to help motivate you into positive action.

Keywords: Father of the Woods, Guardian of Families, protection, strength, stability, luck, money, prosperity, longevity, health, healing, fertility, potency, independence.

Offering: Coins, gemstones, jewelry, ribbons, snowdrops.

Contact: The oak is a tree of Jupiter and Thursday is the day of Jupiter and Thor. For contact visit the Glastonbury oaks Gog and Magog, in Somerset, England. Magog is the tree that still lives and will also be the tree most likely to have a dryad attached to it. Otherwise you can visit any old oak tree, especially if it has a faery ring beneath it, or a grove of oaks.

Approach the dryads and the oakmen with caution as they are shy and retiring creatures. Leave a gift and apologize for intruding.

For the Dagda and Brigid, perform a ritual at the tree. Music is always a good thing particularly that of the harp. Light some incense and a candle color corresponding with your wish or problem (see the color correspondence table at the end of the book).

Lughnasadh is the celebration of the first harvest and is another time suitable for contact with the oak faeries.

The Ash Portal
Otherworldly Power and Healing
Element: Fire/Air with Water

The Ash Tree
The ash tree grows tall into the heavens. Like the oak it is prone

to be struck by lightning. The ash tree is well known over centuries for its healing energies. Most often this was connected with babies and young children, but also with animals.

The ash is known to have been used in magic, especially for wands and staffs. Gwydion the magician, who appears in Celtic mythology in the fourth branch of the Mabinogi, is said to have fashioned his wands from ash, although he did not always put them to good use. Yet there is some protection afforded against enchantment if a person carried ash keys.

Yggdrasil is the World Tree and is thought to be a gigantic ash tree. Odin the All-Father hung from Yggdrasil in a self-sacrificing ritual in search of enlightenment. He took up the runes lying beneath and gained the wisdom and knowledge of them.

The ash tree provides us with healing. It also offers us enlightenment often through self-sacrifice, which can mean giving more and taking less. This does not mean just in a material way, but in others ways, such as giving our time by lending a sympathetic ear, and offering help to those in need. We do not lose by giving in this way but gain something much deeper.

Folklore

Two of the nine realms that make up the Norse Cosmology of Yggdrasil, are Alfheim the home of the light elves, which is situated in the higher region, and Svartalfheim the home of the dark elves or dwarfs, which lies in the middle region and close to Midgard the realm of humankind. Two more realms are Jotunheim the home of the frost giants which is also situated in the middle region and Muspelheim the home of the fire giants which lies in the lower region.

The light elves are fair and beautiful to look at, and are magical creatures who love to dance. They are connected with the heavenly as their realm lies in the higher regions of Yggdrasil. They are benevolent and bestow gifts and have angel-like qualities.

The dark elves or dwarfs are the antithesis of the light elves as they are dark and ugly. They live underground or in darker places in the middle realms of Yggdrasil and are cunning magical goldsmiths and blacksmiths. They are the makers of magical weapons and jewelry but can be malevolent as well as benevolent.

The Frost Giants of Jotunheim are very often benevolent, and are known intermarry.

The Fire Giants of Muspelheim in the lower realms are destined to take part in the devastation of Yggdrasil at Ragnarok.

Dryads or wood nymphs are attached to the ash tree, and these particular ones are the Meliae. The Meliae are daughters of Gaia or Mother Earth and have been linked with the fates and honey-nymphs. The Meliae ash-tree sisters nursed Zeus as a baby and occasionally accompany Pan the Horned God of the forest.

The Ash Portal in a Reading

The ash tree appearing in a reading indicates a sacrifice is necessary in order for you to progress. This progression is both actual and spiritual as they are both connected. If something is wrong in your life, such as constant ill health often due to stress, or sometimes it is the health of another which is a burden, then the ash tree will provide relief. Perhaps you are in the throws of grief or a broken love affair. This is a time of your life that needs to be worked through. The ash will provide speedy recovery, as long as you do your share of work to help in the situation. When you give you receive, though perhaps not at the same time.

The elves and dwarfs cross over from their Otherworld domains that lie close to the world of mortals to aid you. They use the Ash Portal which lies within the faery triad of trees, the oak, ash, and hawthorn, as the swiftest way to do this.

The light elves bring magic, divination, gifts and spiritual insight. They bring relief by gifts of assistance with the suggestion that someone will come into your life to help relieve the burden that is placed upon you. With their help you can formulate new ways, more often spiritual, in which to deal with events and situations. Your intuition is heightened right now, you should learn how to read it, and use it to your advantage.

The dark elves or dwarfs bring creativity and wisdom. They will help you to devise practical ways in which to deal with the events and situations in your life and to view them in a different way.

The frost giants provide strength in adversity. Sometimes you feel abandoned and that no one wants to help or understands your plight. You have the strength within you to break out of the prison you may have made for yourself. Take courage and the bull by the horns and refuse to stay in the prison even though you cannot do much right now to change the current state of affairs.

The fire giants provide motivation and spontaneity, which suggests that motivation has been lacking. Take heart as all will change in not too long a time. Sometimes ideas will come spontaneously to you and you tend to ignore them, now is the time to act.

The Meliae provide nourishment and help in the healing process or road to recovery. They are freer then most dryads and offer you freedom too.

With the Ash Portal you will take a step through into the Otherworld. If there is a blockage in your life, there is hope for the future. This is where the spiritual side of you comes into effect. Deep within you is the ability to see further into your life and gain some well needed optimism. The sun is in sight and a brighter future is foretold. You should look towards it positively and dig deep down inside yourself to discover the answers. Whatever you discover, the Ash Portal represents healing, without and within.

Negative Reading: Between the two types of elves and the two types of giants, you have a mixture or dual balance of both good and evil. When you have more evil or bad luck in your life you need to free the flow of good, or good luck, which may have become blocked. You need to open yourself to the goodness of this world. Having negative feelings towards everything that happens to you can become a habit. This results in attracting further bad luck often resulting in ill health.

Look to your spiritual side for inspiration and enlightenment. This world has more to offer than purely material things. The light elves can help you in this.

Keywords: World Mother, magic, healing energy, prophecy, shaman, astral projection, wisdom, strength, motivation, optimism, spontaneity, divination, freedom, self-sacrifice and inspiration.

Offering: Incense, water, gemstones, small cakes, honey.

Contact: The ash is a tree of the sun and Sunday is the day of the sun. Choose a Sunday for contact. To contact the elves and dwarfs use meditation. Choose a quiet time to sit beneath your ash tree.

If possible choose the faery triad of trees under which to meditate, perhaps not at Samhain or the Summer Solstice as these times will be busy and it can become confusing. Otherwise use a ritual of celebration and offer gifts, especially if you wish to enlist the help of the dark elves or dwarfs, or the frost giants.

Using a visualization exercise will assist you in contact with the light elves. You can do this from home.

Avoid contact with the fire giants as they are too hot to handle!

The Hawthorn Portal
Protection and Good Luck
Element: Fire

The Hawthorn Tree

There are other names for the hawthorn such as mayflower or mayblossom and my mother used to call it the 'bread and cheese tree' and she and her brothers and sisters would eat the young buds and leaves from it on the way to school on the Isle of Man. She would never bring it into the house as it was unlucky to do so.

Lone trees or groves of three or more trees are said to be the most magical. Although known for its *mayblossom*, nowadays the hawthorn blossoms in April or May and occasionally in March. What is now known as The Glastonbury Thorn grows in the abbey grounds there, the original was said to have been planted by Joseph of Arimathea. This thorn tree is unusual as it flowers twice in the year at yuletide and in the spring. The original was cut down in the English Civil War, but the abbey thorn and other hawthorn trees exist at Glastonbury, which are thought to be cuttings of the original tree.

For Druids and pagans in general, the hawthorn is the tree of Bealtaine or Beltane, the May Day spring fertility festival generally celebrated on the eve. Offerings are frequently left at a faery hawthorn on Tara Hill, County Meath, Ireland. I myself paid homage

there.

The hawthorn is one of the trees of the witch. As such, it is usual that the witch uses it for magical purposes.

Folklore

Thomas the Rhymer a thirteenth-century Scottish bard was sitting under the Eildon tree which was thought to be a hawthorn, when he saw a lady riding towards him wearing clothing of grass-green silk and velvet, and with fifty-nine silver bells hanging from her horse's mane. He thought she was the Queen of Heaven but she informed him that she was the Queen of Elfland. He rode away with her on her milk-white horse and after forty days and forty nights they reached the Otherworld where he became her lover. While there, the Queen of Elfland gave him an apple as a reward which in return gave him a tongue that never lied, and the gift of prophecy. He returned to the mortal world after seven years.

The hawthorn is used by pagans on Bealtaine (Beltane). If they are lucky enough to find the tree in blossom, it is used for garlands or on outdoor altars, though some people believe it is all right to bring it indoors on this day only. Placing over doorways brings protection. However, when cutting, avoid lone trees and always leave a gift both to the tree itself and to the faeries of the tree.

As faeries inhabit the tree it is said to be unlucky to cut it down or dig it up. In Ireland there are tales of lone hawthorn trees bleeding or bad luck coming to the folk who destroy them. Roads are generally directed around them and farmers cultivate around them.

There are many associations of this tree with portals or gateways. Cardea is the Roman goddess of health, thresholds, door hinges and door handles. She was given this power by her lover Janus the god of portals and doorways. He had two faces, one to look to the past and one to look to the future. She was said to have used her powers to shut what was open, and to open what was shut. She was a protector especially of children and presides over marriage and childbirth. Her sacred flower is the hawthorn and she was and still is honored at the Bealtaine festival.

The Hawthorn Portal in a Reading

The hawthorn tree is truly magical, as well as providing protection it denotes general good luck and future happiness. In matters of fertility, if you are looking to increase your family or to start one, the time is right for you. Drawing this wand indicates a time for new love, that first exciting phase when you first meet someone and begin a relationship. Enjoy yourself. If it is spring or Bealtaine then ask the hawthorn for permission to take some blossom and put them in your hair or buttonhole. If you are about to be married then, this Portal showing up in a reading is an omen of good luck and future happiness. Again if the tree is in blossom, then slip some hawthorn blossom into your bouquet, buttonhole or hair for added luck.

The Queen of Elfland brings you the gifts of truth and prophecy. Having the gift of truth indicates that people trust you and in you. Your intuition is heightened and you have a good idea of what the future will bring, and therefore can make decisions more easily.

The hawthorn faeries bring all kinds of help to you. Good health is indicated at this time, and if you have been ill, you will now improve. Fertility is at its highest so grasp the opportunity if a business or career opportunity arises, or any other chance in life that can lead to prosperity. If you are about to embark on a new relationship then now is the time to make a move, especially if you have been hesitant. You have the protection of the faery folk so any risk you take is minimized. This might be a time when you will receive justice for any wrong doing against you. See below how to contact the faeries that can help you the most.

The Hawthorn Portal is an exceptionally lucky one; however, it does come with a warning to tread warily. As it is a wand of protection, it does suggest that outside forces are at work for you to require that protection. Someone or something is being a thorn in your side. The protection is a strong one, not many would be able to cross the hedge of thorns without serious injury, so take heart.

The Hawthorn Portal is opening up to you. As the hawthorn lifts its branches to allow you a glimpse of the Otherworld, take the brief opportunity to move forward along your life pathway.

Negative Reading: The Hawthorn Portal is barely affected by the Salamander Wand. Your feelings are slightly suppressed, something is holding you back. All you need is the confidence and courage to take the last tentative step and you will be over the threshold into all that awaits you through the doorway of a new future. The fire of the Hawthorn Portal and the fire of the Salamander will help you with this.

Keywords: Protection, fertility, love, general luck, health, spiritual development, spiritual communication, marriage, justice, strength.

Offering: Ribbons associated with the color of your wish (see the color correspondence table at the end of the book). Also leave gemstones, honey and small cakes.

Contact: The hawthorn is a tree of Mars. Tuesday is the day of Mars or the Norse god Tyr. Choose Tuesday for contact if you are looking for assistance in legal problems or battles of any kind, where you need strength or justice.

The hawthorn is an Otherworld protector, and for me the most mystical of the faery trees. A significant amount of folklore is attached to it, for instance not to take the blossom indoors, or not to cut the tree down or even move it, suggesting that communication with the faeries of this magically powerful tree must be done warily. If it is in the magical triad then the power will be increased threefold. You may even get to see the faeries. If the chance arises, then visit the hawthorns at Tara Hill in County Meath, Ireland or those at Glastonbury in Somerset, England.

The Hawthorn Portal provides magical protection, so keep in contact with those who provide it. As this includes all the species of faeries and not just the Queen of Elfland, you can choose the ones that can help you with your particular problems. Money luck can be helped by the dwarfs, and love and emotions by the mer-people, for general help ask the elves, for good luck the leprechauns, and for matters of the mind, knowledge or wisdom, the sylphs.

Approach the tree at Bealtaine. If the hawthorn is in blossom then it is an even more auspicious time. Sit or lie close to it. You do not have to do much else but make your wish and place your offering. Fertility, protection, or general good luck can be wished for at this time. Other than that, you can approach the tree at twilight (morning or evening) of any day.

The Wands

Earth and Gnomes

The four Wands of Earth — Elm, Elder, Spindle and Blackthorn — are associated with practical issues as demonstrated by the accompanying faeries, Gnomes. Everything earthly belongs to these wands. The ground we walk on and everything we see around us and can touch. These wands relate to the more material side of life, to work and careers, money concerns, home and family life, and general security matters. But they are also forces of stabilization and security.

If we have too much earth then we can be obstinate, rigid and stuck in our ways, materialistic, less in touch with the spiritual side of ourselves, and often lack innovativeness.

Earth people are those born under the signs of Capricorn, Taurus and Virgo.

The Gnomes are hardworking faeries. For centuries they have occupied our homes, farms and barns to lend a helping hand. They and their subgroups also live underground, in forests, caves and mines. Gnomes are guardians and very much connected with nature, encouraging the growth of plants, and care of animals. For centuries there have been sightings of them, and they reside in many countries over the world, so it is not so difficult to make contact with them.

Gnomes exist under many names. They are called the *Kabouter* in the Netherlands, *Tomte* or *Nisse* in Scandinavia, *Gnom* in parts of Eastern

Europe, and the Scottish *Brownie* has similarities, in fact most of Europe and Scandinavia has them. I also have it on authority (from two friends from those parts of the world) that they are to be found in Canada, while *Gnomos* in Argentina are a brownie-like gnome, and *Enanos* are dwarf-like. There have been reported sightings of gnomes for more than two thousand years and in more countries and areas than those listed above.

The other elementals of Earth are the subgroups of gnomes; dwarfs and elves but the dryads and fauns can be included.

Keywords: Material world, humankind, reality, practicality, prosperity, career, physical strength, sexuality, fertility, social activity, nature, domesticity, grounding, life and death.
   Color: Green.

I

The Elm Wand
Metamorphosis
Element: Earth

The Elm Tree

Elm trees grow tall, large and imposing. They have a beautiful shape and are often used to mark boundaries. Unfortunately, many of the older trees, including those with traditions attached to them, have succumbed to Dutch elm disease.

In the Norse creation myth, Odin and his two brothers Vili and Ve found two tree trunks while walking along the sea shore. From this wood they created man and woman. Odin breathed life into them, Vili gave them understanding and emotion, and Ve gave them sight, hearing and speech. The three brothers named the man Ask (from the ash tree and presumably the wood they found), and the woman was named Embla after the elm tree. From Ask and Embla sprang all the races of humankind. They were given Midgard as their home.

Folklore

According to folklore, it is the elves that have a kinship with the elm tree. The elm is a tree of the Celtic Underworld or Otherworld and guardian of the dead, and a tree of faery raths or burial mounds. The elves are sometimes human sized but can also be much smaller and in Norse mythology they are referred to as *light* and *dark*. The light elves are beautiful to look at but the dark elves are ugly and as dark as pitch and are more associated with dwarfs.

The elves we talk about here are both light and dark. The light elves are connected with beauty, calmness, guardianship and gifts. The dark elves are connected with the hard work and creativity of the crafts and magic. But both types of elves can be helpful to you.

The Elm Wand in a Reading

Similar to the yew tree in a number of qualities, the elm tree indicates great change in your life. The changes can be welcomed or forced upon you. The change can be within you as a person, meaning you are about to undergo a complete metamorphosis, a recreating of yourself. It can also be an outside force in that your whole world has or will turn topsy-turvy and you have to begin again. Do not despair, for just as when the caterpillar changes into a butterfly, this will lead to a more beautiful and fresh existence. Hold your head up and stand fast like the elm. The elm is not a fighter or leader but a stalwart companion there to support you.

The elves will ensure you retain your dignity during the

transitional phase. They react more to people who try to help themselves and go with the flow of change rather than resist it or those who stand around and wait for something to happen. They will reward hard work while remaining compassionate to your predicament or trials, bringing you good luck for the future.

The Elm Wand also signifies primordial female power. This power comes from Embla the first woman. Change cannot be avoided but indeed is more often welcomed; however, this inherent power resides within you whether you are woman or man, providing you with strength and endurance.

Through hard work metamorphosis is accomplished, and although occasionally it is not the happiest of circumstances that has prompted the change, it will lead to a better and more fulfilling life pathway.

Negative Reading: You are in denial and are resisting the natural forces of change. Look deep inside yourself for the truth is there, and you need to accept it. Sooner or later we all have to let go, especially if something or someone has already let go of us. Open up to the infinite possibilities, there is a whole new and wonderful life out there waiting to surprise you. Do not give up so easily. You are not at a crossroads so take the pathway forward. For help to do this contact the elves, you already have the strength even if you do not yet realize it.

Keywords: Metamorphosis, transition, death, birth, rebirth, cycles of life, dignity, mother, grandmother, strength, stability, loyalty, wisdom, protection, endurance, empathy and compassion.

Offering: Milk, mead, gemstones, flute music

Contact: The elm is a tree of Saturn. Choose Saturday for contact possibly outdoors in an elm grove. If you cannot find an elm grove, sit beneath a lone elm. Samhain is the Celtic New Year and a time for the old year to die and the new one to begin, so this festival is a good time to make your wishes for the future. Try singing, humming, or playing a musical instrument, particularly the flute, but if you feel uncomfortable with this, then sing a tune in your head while meditating. Ask for help in periods of major change, or self-metamorphosis.

The Elder Wand
Protection and Abundance
Element: Earth with Water

The Elder Tree
The elder has long been used as a protector of homes and animals. It wards away evil spirits and negative energy. Witches are said to be able to turn themselves into elder trees. The Rollright Stones, an ancient stone circle in Oxfordshire, England have a legend attached to them. The history of these ancient stones records a king who tried to conquer England and was turned into a stone by a witch (The King Stone), along with his men (The King's Men Stones), and his knights (The Whispering Knights). The witch turned herself into an elder tree. If the tree is cut while in blossom, rather like the Hawthorn, it is said to bleed.

The elder tree gives beautiful pungent white blossom and delicious fruit which has long been used in remedies and wine making. The blossom has a narcotic scent and musical instruments are made from its wood.

Folklore
The Hyldemoer or Elder Mother appears in a story by Hans Anderson, (English translation: 'The Elder-Tree Mother' or 'Little

Elder-Tree Mother'). She is a friendly soul but can be tricky if you harm her tree. Take care if you cut down an elder for the wood, especially for making cradles as Hyldemoer will haunt your house and torment your baby. Ask permission of her first for using the wood for any other purpose. Cutting down this tree as with the Hawthorn is said to be unwise. The Hyldemoer figure exists in other cultures often with a similar name and it appears they are one and the same faery.

Faeries are said to live beneath the Rollright Stones and come out at midnight to joyfully dance around them in the moonlight.

Gnomes are protectors and look after and protect animals of all kind, whether domestic or wild. They protect plants and encourage growth.

The elder tree could well be another faery portal, and it is on Midsummer's Eve or the Summer Solstice that you are more likely to see the faeries that use it.

The Elder Wand in a Reading

When the Elder Wand appears in a reading you can be sure that magical forces are at work. The elder tree is earth with water and this means that some emotions are involved. It indicates that you have a challenge in your life. This could be in your dealings with other people. The challenge might be in you resolutely sticking to an important principle that someone is pressurizing you to break, or someone could be attempting to spoil or interfere with your plans. This can be upsetting and unsettling. The elder is there to help and protect what is yours, so take heart. You do not need to defend yourself, just persevere and time will show you are right. Any true negativity towards you is repelled by the elder.

The Hyldemoer is not subtle when it comes to seeking retribution for harm done to what she considers hers, though she means no real harm. Just like anyone else she insists on respect. In this way she is showing you that you are also entitled to respect. To be firm yet kind is the best way forward. She is generous and shares freely what is hers as long as people appreciate it. In the same way, although you should guard what is yours, you also need to share all that is superfluous to your needs.

The gnomes as protectors of animals are on hand to protect you and what is yours. In times of old, animals were used as currency. You can share excess wealth of something without worry that what you wish to keep will be lost, especially if you have worked hard for it.

The Elder Wand shows you that you are at the present time going through, or are soon to approach, a prosperous time. You have an abundance of something, more than you need or is of use to you (not necessarily of material things). However, it could be that others see this, and perhaps expect too much. This is a time to be generous without letting others take advantage. If others are not happy with that, or with what you are offering, then you should insist on respect for what is your good fortune and if they are not grateful for the opportunities you offer, then it is their loss.

Negative Reading: You are being selfish and unnecessarily hoarding. You are over protecting what is yours. Perhaps this is because in the past you have been disadvantaged in some way. It should not be a case, of 'this is my time for luck, you will get yours sometime', or 'do not steal my thunder' it is more of rejoicing in your good fortune and sharing some of it. Good fortune rubs off onto others, and seeing someone else happy makes it all the more enjoyable.

Keywords: Protection, abundance, good fortune, prosperity, challenges, repelling of negative forces, joy, benevolence, generosity.

Offering: Water, collect litter.

Contact: The elder is a tree of Venus. Friday is the day of Venus and also of Freyja and Frigg. Freyja and Frigg are associated with the elder, and like Venus their day is also Friday and it is from where the name 'Friday' actually derives.

Approach this tree with caution, show respect for it. You can do this by giving a gift of water, or collecting litter. Fallen branches around it can be collected for making wands but still be sure to leave a gift. Contact the Hyldemoer to ask for protection and support and also be sure to ask permission if you wish to take a small piece of wood or wand from the tree, or any of its fruits.

Midsummer Eve/ Summer Solstice, is the most potent time to have contact with the Hyldemoer, Gnomes and faeries in general.

The Spindle Wand
Web of Fate, Benevolence and Industry
Element: Earth

The Spindle Tree

The evergreen spindle tree grows on chalky soils and often in the hedgerows. A small but very useful tree, the wood has been used for centuries in the making of spindles. The wood is also excellent for making artists charcoal, and the seeds make a yellow dye. In the waning year it is a beautiful sight of crimson leaves (changing from its mid-green), and rose red or bright pink fruits with orange seeds. However, the scent from the tree is not pleasant and its fruits are poisonous.

The Botanical name of the tree *Euonymus europaeus* and is

associated with the *Furies* or *Erinyes*, the Roman and Greek supernatural creatures or three goddesses of vengeance, who are renowned for being cruel but fair. The three women were avengers of crime, particularly that of matricide and patricide, and crimes of rule and law breaking. They were portrayed as ugly winged women, entwined with serpents.

Folklore

Through the use of its wood as a spindle, the spindle tree has associations with the triple goddess. The Roman *Furies* or Greek *Erinyes* are a triple goddess (that is three goddesses who work as one), along with the Norse *Norns,* and Greek *Fates* or *Moirai* (*Moirae*) and *Graces*. *Brigid* and the *Morrigan* are also thought to be triple goddesses. Single goddesses can also have triple aspects. In modern times, the triple goddess is generally viewed as the archetypal maiden, mother and crone.

The triple goddess is often associated with fate particularly the Norns. These goddesses weave the web or tapestry of fate. One represents *that which has become* or the past, one represents *that which is becoming* or the present, and one represents *that which will be* or the future. The *Norns* determine the future of gods and man alike.

The triple goddess is linked with the three faery queens or faery godmothers who are benevolent. These faery godmothers often appear after the birth of a baby.

The three faery queens or godmothers make a frequent appearance in mythology and folklore. In Arthurian legend, mortally wounded King Arthur was rowed away on a barge by three faery queens (depending on the particular myth) to Avalon.

Frau Holda (Holle, Huldra) is the faery patron of spinning and weaving. She is the good Faery Godmother's equivalent. She regularly appears during the twelve days of Christmas. She rewards hard work and industry. As many faery queens do, she can appear in two forms, one an old woman with crooked teeth and nose, and one a beautiful young woman all dressed in white.

The Spindle Wand in a Reading

The spindle tree in a reading shows three things, industry, benevolence, and the weaving of the web of fate.

First is industry as the spindle, made of spindle wood, is a symbol of work. The spindle tree in your reading indicates that you will have to work hard to achieve results. The work is often difficult and can cause minor harm. This does not mean purely in the pricking of a finger, but the work can also make you tired and achy. So the work is not easy. Consequently there is difficult and hard work ahead of you.

However, this is rewarded by the three faery queens and Frau Holda. They are there to reward you after the work is done. They appreciate the effort you have put in and the results are that you receive recognition in the way of a gift or great success. If you are embarking on a new project right now, the hard work ahead will prove fruitful in the long run. You have the blessing of the faery queens and Frau Holda.

The Spindle Wand indicates that you cannot change past actions, but in weaving your web you can change the present as it is in constant flux. In doing so, you alter the future which is still to be determined (but is transformable). You may have regrets about the past, yet you can do little to change it. When you weave your web of life, it is rather intricate and every action you take is interrelated and affects your future. So although you cannot change the past you can do your best to make amends (which would certainly please the *Furies*), in the present you can be careful what actions you take and diligently or thoughtfully plan before acting, knowing that every action will affect your future.

Remember that industry, benevolence and weaving of the web of fate are interrelated.

Negative Reading: You are stuck in a rut and lamenting the position in which you now find yourself. However, you are somewhat to blame for this. Taking a different pathway may have changed things but you know this and now regret it. To move forward you need to stop living in the past and make new and thoughtful plans for your future. This is not beyond you, like you may think, but is in your power. To change things in our lives we have to work at it so seek advice if necessary. Have a cleansing bath in salt and herbs or cleansing oils such as Frankincense or Lavender.

Keywords: Fate, benevolence, industry, blessing, weaving, crafts, regret, hard work, diligent or thoughtful planning, gifts, reward, fruitfulness, success.

Offering: Ribbons, something you have put together or made yourself, corn dolly.

Contact: Appeal to the three faery queens especially if you have a negative wand. Otherwise ask for strength. Talk directly to them, tell them all that you have planned, or if you are stuck in a rut and need inspiration.

For contact of Frau Holda, Christmas Eve until twelfth night is a good time along with the Winter Solstice/Yule and Lughnasadh. If it is not close to this time of year then try either a Wednesday (Odin's Day) or Friday (Frigg's Day).

The festival of Lughnasadh is a good time to contact the faeries especially in regards to rewards, as this is the time of year for rest after hard work.

The Blackthorn Wand
Adversity with Protection
Element: Earth with Fire

The Blackthorn Tree

The blackthorn tree is thornier than the hawthorn. And while the hawthorn is a tree which brings luck, the blackthorn has more negative connotations. The branches are dense and it makes a good hedge of protection to guard boundaries of property. The flowers appear first with this tree bringing beauty to the dark winter, and make it easily distinguishable from the hawthorn. The wood has been used for many things including the Irish shillelagh (used to fight) and magic wands, making it a magical tree. The blackthorn fruit (the sloe) is used in cooking and to make sloe gin, my mother used to make this every year.

In the past, the blackthorn has received much bad press as a tree of black magic by the Christian Church. It does however, as a *black* thorn, have connotations of absorbance and the dispersing of negative energy. The blackthorn is representative of the waning moon and year but when the first signs of spring appear, blackthorn is there to brighten us with its blossom, suggesting it is more representative of the waning moon and waning year leading up to the New Moon and spring.

Folklore

In faery tales the blackthorn appears as the impenetrable hedge or thicket around the castle where Sleeping Beauty lays sleeping. All those who try to pass through it are caught up and lose their lives, except of course the handsome prince who only manages it after the hundred years of curse has passed. Sleeping Beauty was doomed to die but the curse was lessened in its severity by the good Faery Godmother.

As with the hawthorn, the blackthorn is a sacred faery tree. The Irish tribe of faeries the Lunantishee, guard the blackthorn, and it is unlucky to cut a branch from it on either May 11th, or November 11th. If you do so, misfortune will ensue. The blackthorn is a possible protection tree of a faery portal, especially if you find it close to the oak or ash trees.

The Blackthorn Wand in a Reading

The blackthorn tree indicates a thorny time in your life as it is earth with fire, which could mean passion and a fiery intensity is involved. However, it is not all doom and gloom as spring follows winter and a new and magical moon will soon appear. In the meantime, weather the storm and try to calm the situation and not react so passionately. Sit it out until spring comes and try not to get too agitated. Outside influences could be causing the problem. Someone or something is literally being a thorn in your side. Yet, the thorn is also protective and you can use it to your own advantage.

You are protected by the Faery Godmother. The end of a phase is in sight and a new one will soon begin. The Lunantishee adds to that protection and guard you from any real harm. This is an uncomfortable phase you are currently going through and life is difficult and you will need to focus on the coming good times, knowing that the Faery Godmother will lessen the impact of your troubles.

The Blackthorn Wand means strife but protection. You feel you are being attacked. There is a possibility that this will pass rather like the nine day wonder. This attack could be linked to sexual activity. Perhaps you feel your relationship is built on this alone, or perhaps you have difficulties with sexual compatibility.

Mentally build a hedge around yourself and believe no harm can pass through it. Try calming exercises, deep breathing, meditation and visualization. Negativity will be dispersed and this in itself lessens impact. Use cleansing and protective herbs and oils, perhaps frankincense, lavender, salt, black pepper, juniper, sandalwood, and obsidian and smoky quartz gemstones.

Negative Reading: You are letting the situation spiral out of control. You cannot see any way out of your troubles and perhaps think it is your lot to suffer. It is not. Use your intuition, something is telling you what to do and how to react. Try not to be a martyr to your troubles. This phase will end even if you cannot see it. Try to break through the fog that surrounds you and put up your protective hedge. Be assured that if you do, you will feel more secure.

Keywords: Adversity, protection, strife, troubles, attack, fiery passion, sexual activity, light, spring, new moon, end phase.

Offering: Fruit perhaps berries or apples, ribbons, gemstones.

Contact: The Faery Godmother and Lunantishee are best contacted on Samhain, Bealtaine, and the Spring and Autumn Equinoxes. Twilight is also a good time along with the New Moon period.

Air and Sylphs

The four Wands of Air are the Beech, Fir, Aspen and Cherry and the sylphs are the accompanying elemental spirit. Sylphs deal with the intellect, knowledge, thinking, ideas and creativity, but also to sociability and communication. These aspects are associated with the waking conscious, and this means we are aware of our thoughts and actions. Too much air can lead us to an excess of day dreaming, and metaphorically being *away with the faeries*.

Air people are those born under the signs of Aquarius, Gemini and Libra.

Sylphs are the ethereal faeries of air and are sometimes said to be spirits. They are highly evolved and angel-like beings who are generally beautiful to look at. They charm man and beast alike. Although many sources portray them as having wings, the one I

saw did not have any but glided through the air. Owing to their wraithlike forms they find it easier than other faery species to cross through the veil separating the worlds. Music is important to them and they love to sing and dance. They live for centuries and have the wisdom of those years.

Ariel in Shakespeare's *The Tempest* is Prospero's familiar spirit and a sylph. He is imprisoned in a pine tree by a sorceress or evil witch. Ariel is a good faery who refused to commit evil deeds and so angered the sorceress. Ariel was eventually freed by Prospero.

Keywords: Wisdom, knowledge, truth, perception, intuition, thought, communication, conflicts both inner and outer, harmony, art, poet, writer, guidance, inspiration, divination.
   Color: Yellow

The Beech Wand
Writing, Wisdom, Communication,
Element: Air with Earth

The Beech Tree

The beech tree often called 'the mother of the woods' can grow to great heights and girth, and stands impressive and proud. As they grow older, beech trees occasionally develop hollows in the trunk. Its leaves in spring are a beautiful fresh green which darken as the year progresses finally turning to gold and copper in the autumn months. Beech is commonly used for hedging, as the young beech retains its autumn bronze leaves all winter until

replaced by the new leaves in spring.

The beech is a source of forest food and is loved by deer. In the past, it was often used to inscribe on and is one of the first woods to be used for writing, and later to make paper.

At Avebury stone circle in Wiltshire UK, there are some beeches which grow on tumuli or burial mounds which attract pagans. Also at Avebury is what is known as the *Tolkien Trees*, which are said to have inspired Tolkien to write Lord of the Rings. They lie by the East Gate where the roots entwine all over the bank. And Tennyson described the beech tree as the 'serpent-rooted beech' in his poem *The Brook*.

Folklore

The faery Ogma, also a Celtic god, was as strong as Hercules and credited with inventing the Ogham Alphabet. The alphabet was likely to have been carved on beech as it was a popular tree for carving upon in ancient times. The Ogma is said to be the son of Brigid and grandson or son of the Dagda. He is gifted with bardic eloquence and is rather an enigma as not much has been written about him.

There is an old custom concerning the beech tree and wishing sticks. A twig of beech wood was wished upon and left in the beech tree or pushed into the earth beneath it. The faeries would find the stick and take it into the Otherworld where they would debate upon whether or not the wish should be granted.

The Beech Wand in a Reading

With the beech tree you have both the power of communication and eloquence to help you, not just through difficult or trying times (perhaps in matters of finance), but also in launching new projects. You have the capacity to make that communication work, and the beech's strength and endurance to see projects through to completion. The earth side of this tree will help you in the practical matters.

Ogma is there guiding you. You may have a learning process to work through, or perhaps are already taking part in or are soon to be taking part in an educational course of some sort. It could be you are a new teacher or have a career which includes public speaking. Ogma is there for you in all of this and also provides you with extra strength to help you cope with the pressure both physically and mentally.

The wishing faeries are there to add luck to the proceedings.

The Beech Wand indicates a successful time in which a mentor might be concerned. You will progress and succeed as you have the gift of speech. If you are a writer, poet or follow any sort of artistic pursuit, you are blessed with inspiration and productiveness. Any mental blockages or stage fright will improve from this time onwards. Take advantage of this time to move forward.

Negative Reading: You do have the powers of eloquence but do not use them. You lack confidence in your abilities. Perhaps in the past you have been put down or told you had nothing good to say. You need to break through this barrier and tell yourself, perhaps through affirmation and help from the faeries, that you do have the power of communication. You could be a frustrated writer or artist, who lacks confidence. Now is the time for you to learn to work harder, as you will not be successful unless you work at it and finish projects.

Keywords: Communication, writing, the arts, wisdom, learning, eloquence.

Offering: Water, gemstones, small cakes.

Contact: The beech is a tree of Saturn. Find a fallen twig beneath a beech tree and carve your initials on it. Return it to the tree, perhaps on a Saturday, and make your wish before pushing it into the ground at the tree base, and if possible among the roots. If you are lucky the faeries will look favorably upon you.

Speak to Ogma at the beech tree on a Wednesday, the day of communication. The wishing faeries can be contacted on the New Moon. Otherwise Imbolg is another day you can present yourself at the tree as Ogma is the son of Brigid and she in turn is the patron of poets. Between them they will help you if you lack that extra bit of push you need to get started.

The Fir Wand
Clear Vision, Perspective, Enlightenment
Element: Air

The Fir Tree
The fir tree is an evergreen tree from the conifer family. The fir cone opens and closes depending on whether it is sunny or raining. Firs are tall trees reaching high into the heavens, and can see over the heads of many others and far into the distance. The fir tree is also connected with second sight.

As the Christmas tree, the fir is often short lived and cut down in its prime to shine and glitter and give pleasure to all.

The fir tree has associations with the Greek god Pan, and also the satyr who chases dryads.

Folklore
Although the fir is a tree of air it does have a connection with the King of the Dwarfs who appears in a tale in which fir cones turn to silver.

The Christmas tree faery, who graces the upper branches, is the sylph, the angel-like faery being. Sylphs fly as high as the fir tree top soaring in and out of the topmost branches. Being so highly evolved and having the best view of everything in existence of all the faeries, the sylph has the gift of second sight and wisdom, and can pass easily through the veil separating the Otherworld from the world of mortals.

The Fir Wand in a Reading

The tall fir gives you clear sight. You have the ability to see beyond the beyond, to spot something that normally would be missed. This ability comes from within and is the power to see everything in a new light bringing enlightenment and a new awareness of what is really going on around you. With this gift, life ahead will appear as a brand new sunny day in which anything is possible. You know that other people have this gift and with it they progress, and now it is your turn.

The sylphs will assist you in tapping into previously unused parts of your psyche. They will leave signs to help you in this, look out for them. You will progress in spiritual awareness. Spiritual awareness is a personal thing and each person reaches it in a different way. The sylph will help you retain your individuality and not be too much led by others. Think what you want out of life and go forth with a new optimism that the future will be different.

The King of Dwarfs will be hovering in the background to ensure that you stay on earth and not gain so much air and enlightenment that you forget to live and prosper.

With the Fir Wand you will reach new heights. You are now likely to embark on a different pathway in life. A brilliant light illuminates this pathway. At first you may be unsure of yourself, but do not worry as you will work on it using your intuition and it will soon become clear to you. Perception is a gift that makes us see the world in a different way. Look around you, normally you might take things at face value or see only what is on the surface. Look now at what you would normally miss or ignore. Seek the deeper aspects of things and look for the symbols or indicators which will guide you on your way.

Negative Reading: You are seeing everything in black and white. You have an 'if you cannot see it, then it does not exist' attitude. Alternatively, you might close your mind to new possibilities and understanding. This will leave you in the darkness feeling bewildered or pessimistic and with a defeatist attitude. Open your eyes and mind, there is so much out there that you are missing. Climb to a higher height for a birds-eye view, and see how much more you can see from up there, than you can down on the ground. Without clear vision you miss much in life. You are far too grounded in reality. Add a little air to your earth. You can only benefit from it.

Keywords: Clear vision, perception, enlightenment, second sight, wisdom, intuition, individuality, optimism, illumination.

Offering: Feathers, incense, bubbles and gemstones.

Contact: Imbolg, Spring Equinox, Bealtaine, dawn and also the New Moon, are good times for contact. Find a fir tree and look up into the branches. See how high it reaches. Imagine you are a sylph gliding among its branches or sitting on the highest branch. How much can you see from up there? The sylph will help you use this new perception within your own life. The feather and incense represent air. When you light the incense, or alternatively blow bubbles as high as you can (you can buy them in children's toy shops), let the incense smoke or the bubbles take your wish of assistance to the sylphs. Remember to leave some gemstones or a shiny gift for the King of Dwarfs to help you keep you grounded, especially if astrologically you are under the influence of the element of air.

The Aspen Wand
Astral Travel, Voice
Element: Air

The Aspen Tree
The graceful aspen tree is famous for its quivering or trembling leaves, even when all other trees are still. As it does so, it whispers. The aspen is a unisexual tree and has a pale gray slender trunk, its leaves bud first as copper, turning to bright green in the summer and to gold or bright yellow in the winter.

Its wood was used as a defensive shield. This is a defense against psychic as well as physical harm. The aspen is a tree favored by animals as fodder; among them are the deer, goat and sheep.

Folklore
The aspen belongs to the poplar family and is a tree of the spirit. In medieval times the poplar bud or leaf was used in flying ointment. This means it provides passage into the Otherworld in a shamanistic way or by astral travel. It allows the user to come and go safely.

The Faery Queen waits by the aspen tree to offer the gift of voice to those who deserve it. The leaf is placed under the tongue to achieve this. More than one faery queen lives in the Otherworld and each has her own special or magical abilities.

The Aspen Wand in a Reading
Listen with patience using your intuition to what the aspen has

to tell you. A message awaits you. This message heralds duality. If you are in the dark it heralds light, or if you feel vulnerable you will be shielded and gain a feeling of invincibility, or if you feel lacking in voice you will now be able to express yourself. First discover what the message is, then act on it. If you already have a shamanic gift or can travel on the astral plain, use it to seek advice. If not, try meditating or visualizing. Now is the time for you to gain new insight. If this wand appears in the same reading as the Fir Wand, then you have the ability to progress quickly, otherwise be patient as your time will come.

The Faery Queen offers the gift of speech or voice. You will discover that people will listen to you. If you have had a problem communicating then you will now be able to voice your opinions in an eloquent way. Make sure that you use this gift, but not over use it to the point of dominance or arrogance, and you will keep the gift for as long as you wish. With voice you can express yourself in new ways.

The Aspen Wand indicates passage into the Otherworld in one way or another, through meditation, through intuition, or through secret messages or shamanism. You can gain much from using your spiritual side. Take time out for contemplation. Locked inside you is knowledge of the future. If you were seeking answers or a new life pathway, then you will soon receive messages of guidance. If you doubt your ability, perhaps as a teacher, speaker, writer or musician, you will gain your own distinctive voice.

Negative Reading: There are indications of one or other of the following problems. You have a mental blockage or are too influenced by others. This prevents you from finding your own voice and you are too often led rather than a leader. You do not have to be a leader, just an individual. Perhaps you feel too stuck in your ways to change, and yet the ability is there. Look deep inside yourself and open your mind to the possibilities. Beware of arrogance or dominance over others if you already *feel* you have found a voice, for being too opinionated leads to narrow-mindedness. Being too individualistic separates you from others; you can be an individual yet still be part of a team.

Keywords: Astral Travel, voice, defense, shield, shamanism, eloquence, individuality, duality, progress, intuition, contemplation, guidance, writer, poet, musician.

Offering: Music, perhaps a drum or tinkling bells or other percussion instrument, played rhythmically and softly.

Contact: Meditating beneath the tree is the best way to go about contacting those in the Otherworld. The quivering and whispering of the aspen leaves have a hypnotic effect and make meditation easier. Do this preferably on a sunny summer or spring day with a breeze. If your appeal is to the Faery Queen, then place an aspen leaf or bud beneath your tongue before meditation, and remove afterwards. The month of May is a good time for requests. Bealtaine and the Summer Solstice are perfect times for contact.

The Cherry Wand
Warrior, Transformation
Element: Air

Cherry! Dearest Cherry!
Higher lift thy branches,
Under which the Vilas
Dance their magic roundels.
Translation by Thomas Keightley from the *Wiener Jahrbucher*

The Cherry Tree

The fruit of the cherry tree is good for you, and of course the spring blossom is most beautiful and fragrant. The cherry tree has been used for divining especially in connection with the cuckoo.

Communication with the tree itself is known. Some Japanese folk tales portray the cherry tree as a tree of life and death. A human life is given so another might live, or a human life is given so the tree might live on. Tales of the Virgin Mothers of Buddha and Jesus relate how they were both nourished by the cherry tree during their pregnancies, in which the cherry tree lowers its branches so its fruit can be reached.

The tree also signifies moral strength as told in the tale of how George Washington having cut down his father's favorite cherry had the moral strength to admit it was he.

Folklore

The Vilas are the sylphs who dance beneath the cherry tree. Vilas have been known to harm humans if they are disturbed and are likely to shoot arrows at you. The Vilas are Serbian faeries or nymph-like creatures who live in the mountains, hills, forests and trees. Young, beautiful and dressed in white they are a sight to behold. Their friends are the stags, but they are said to be fierce warriors. They can rise up in the air and sometimes live in the clouds. Shape-shifting is one of their talents and the Vilas will shape-shift into a swan, snake or falcon. They also have the power of prophecy. Vilas have been known to marry humans.

The Cherry Wand in a Reading

The cherry tree is magical tree and one of divination. You have the power to use your intuition in all matters of the mind and inner conflicts. And there is conflict at the present time. This can be personal or involve others. You might be feeling weak and helpless and about to give up, but this period will be short-lived.

Dig deep inside yourself and you will see you do have the power of foresight and prophecy. You already have an idea of how things are going to be, so do not try to discard it just because the moment is a challenging one.

If you are creative, the Vilas will be naturally attracted to you and will help you overcome mental blockages, and inspire you with new ideas. They will also assist you in conflicts. The Vilas will help you add balance and compromise in disputes so the difficulties can be overcome without you losing face or becoming weak. Transformation is a key word. A stronger and better you is possible.

The Cherry Wand is the warrior wand and a wand of inner strength. You have the ability to battle with finesse, not physically, but mentally and through this you will gain wisdom. When the Cherry Wand appears in a cast or spread, it indicates that you have the strength to overcome obstacles or blockages and a happier clearer way lies ahead of you. Any problems will be short lived so do not give up easily. You have the strength to make informative decisions and do the right thing. A sacrifice might be necessary to allow for regeneration. A new phase is ahead. Something might have to change, but your intuition will tell you what that is. Nothing is as bad as you had imagined.

Negative Reading: You are not opening yourself up to the possibilities. You have closed yourself off and this weakens you. You cannot live on dreams. Do not hide from the truth, face up to worries and call on the Vilas to provide you with inner strength and wisdom. Guilt weighs heavy. Sometimes it is best to own up as long as it does not ruin the life of another. In that case you should bear the burden and move on with the knowledge that you have learnt by your mistakes.

Keywords: Warrior, transformation, regeneration, prophecy, divination, intuition, foresight, conflict, balance, compromise, moral strength, sacrifice, creativity, inspiration and wisdom.

Offering: Small cakes, flowers, fruits or pretty objects.

Contact: As a tree of Venus contact can be made on a Friday and the color of white or pale pink can be worn. Meditate indoors or make wishes outdoors while looking up at cirrus clouds. Cirrus comes from the Latin 'curl of hair' and they are those high clouds that look fine and wispy or feathery. See if you can see the sylphs in their shapes. Ask for help to clear blockages and to gain inspiration, perhaps so you can remove yourself from predicaments. This tree has the power of regeneration. The Spring Equinox is a time for inspiration and balance. You can use your favorite form of divining, perhaps this oracle, while sitting beneath the tree for improved insight.

Water and the Undines

The Wands of Water, Apple, Birch, Willow and Hazel, as the undines will show, cover the emotions and feelings. They relate to love and relationships, passion and compassion, and intuitiveness. Although the waters can be calm and peaceful, too much water can lead to an excess of emotion flowing, resulting in loss of control and turbulence in our lives. Water can assist in healing and you may have heard the term 'healing waters'.

Water people are those born under the signs of Pisces, Cancer and Scorpio.

Undines are the elementals of water or a water spirit. Water spirits are found in any body of water, the ocean, lakes, rivers, waterfalls, pools and streams. They often control the flow of this water. They are human-like sexual creatures and many water spirits are on the look out for a sexual partner. They can be beautiful but dangerous beings and when dealing with them it is best to apply caution. Water spirits often have the power of  healing and knowledge of herbs and herbal remedies. Contact with them can be by psychic means.

Keywords: Emotions, feelings, healing, beauty, music, birth, knowledge, fertility, inspiration, optimism, choice, nurture.
Color: Blue

1

The Apple Wand
Passionate Love, Wholeness, Forfeit, Choice
Element: Water with Air

The Apple Tree

The ancient apple tree can be both wild and cultivated with a variety of flavors from the sour crab and cooking apples to the dessert apples with many other apple tastes in between. In the spring the fragrant blossom fills the trees. The world would be a sadder place without the humble, but noble apple.

John Chapman otherwise known as Johnny Appleseed was a pioneer in the planting of apple trees in the US. He became a legend after traipsing the countryside during his lifetime dressed in the coarsest of clothing and barefoot. He planted small nurseries of apple trees for the local folk, Europeans and Native Americans alike, so that none should go hungry. He was truly a saint.

Many traditional customs involve the apple. Sadly, not as many people follow these customs now.

Folklore

The apple tree is a magical tree connected to the Otherworld and appears more frequently in folklore than perhaps any other tree, often taking an important part. Glastonbury's Avalon is called 'The Isle of Apples'. Linked to Avalon is the faery, Morgan Le Fey or Morgana. King Arthur was taken to the Isle of Avalon by the three faery queens when he was mortally wounded.

The apple is very much connected with the Celtic festival

Samhain and many customs accompany the fruit for this day. Samhain is a time of year when the veil between the Otherworld and world of mortals is thin.

The apple also features in faery tales as with Snow White. The wicked queen tricks Snow White with the poisoned but beautifully delicious and innocent looking apple.

The apple is the fruit of the Otherworld. As I have explained in the Hawthorn Portal above, one was given to Thomas the Rhymer by the Queen of Elfland and this gave him the gift of prophecy and a tongue that never lied. The apple of course appears in the story of Adam and Eve, and reflections of this story can be found in the mythology of many other cultures.

There is a Celtic myth associated with the apple. In this tale, a strange faery maiden appears to *Connla*, the son of *Conn* of the hundred fights (or battles) and only he can see her. She tells him she comes from a faery mound and is in love with him and wishes to take him back with her. Hearing this, Conn the king wanting to prevent it, asks for help from his Druid counsel who makes a charm. The charm causes the faery maiden to disappear, but before doing so she throws Connla a magic apple. For a whole month the apple is all Connla can eat or wishes to eat as he so longs for the maiden. At last she returns and they sail away together and are never seen again.

As you can see, the apple appears to be used as an enchanted weapon of seduction. It entices people with its delicious beauty (as in the faery tale Snow White) and is used as a symbol of sexual lust (the eating of the forbidden fruit), or the luring away of a man by a beautiful woman who promises much but for this he has to give up his previous and normal life.

Sirens are linked with the seas, and are seductresses often luring the sailor to his death. They tempt not only the flesh— often with song — but the spirit, and in that way are also linked to air.

Undines are water nymphs. Water nymphs are renowned for

falling in love with mortals and come into the mortal world and so forfeiting their own way of life and often not being able to return.

The Apple Wand in a Reading

The apple tree brings wholeness. You have much for which to be thankful. During this time of wholeness, it is easy to be seduced by outside influences, by beauty and the promise of a better life. This is sometimes linked with passionate love. Passionate love can blind the eyes and stop you from seeing the world around you. Often at this time there is a choice to be made and that choice may mean a forfeit or giving up of something. This forfeit perhaps involves something stable (but mundane), which needs to be sacrificed for something that is more of a gamble or calculated risk (but is exciting). This does not mean the choice is wrong, however, it should be well thought out. The apple brings you a gift of prophecy. Listen to any warnings that come from deep within you which you are likely to be ignoring. You cannot lie to yourself, so face up to truths.

The faery maiden or Queen of Efland and the three faery queens linked with fate, are your connections to the Apple Wand.

The faery maiden seduces you with her beautiful and delicious but enchanted apple. She brings excitement and passion into your life, yet you still have a choice. As the Queen of Elfland, who is also a seducer, she rewards you with her gift of prophecy enabling you to make a better choice.

The three faery queens happily weave together the threads of life you are making and add them to your life tapestry or web. Once something is done it can not be undone.

The Sirens bring a warning of potential danger or risk, while the Undines and water nymphs bring a warning of regret in the longing for the former life.

The Apple Wand portends a happy and exciting time of life. Excitement and a new pathway lie ahead. Whether this pathway is the right one for you lies in the hands of fate. You are the driver behind that fate as we weave our own web along the way, even if it is affected by many inner and outer influences past and present. The choice you have to make appears urgent. You are eager to go forward, however take time out to rest, think and contemplate on what this all means. Letting the initial excitement die away into something more tangible, will help to ensure that this is the right pathway to take. Listen to your intuition and what messages it is attempting to give you. What you forfeit one day might be regretted or you might miss your former life, or perhaps will not, only time will tell. Passion is not the only thing that can cause lust and blind us from reality. Other exciting events such as material things, career, moving house (or country), travel and more, can also be the cause of a choice that has to be made.

Negative Reading: Problems of your past are repeating themselves. You are well and truly blinded. You are not listening to the warnings within and are deceiving yourself. The risk you take is not a calculated one. Take a long hard look at yourself and what is around you. Try to take time out to reflect. Once you are on the wrong pathway it will be hard or impossible to return to your old life. In this case, are you prepared if everything should go wrong? You should be.

It could be that change in your life is inevitable or change is necessary. Think carefully on how you should go about this. Water with air can leave you too high in the clouds emotionally. The feeling of being on cloud nine will not last forever, sooner or later the clouds will clear and you may be left with the harsh reality of the situation. Watch out that you do not come back down to earth with a bump.

Keywords: Passionate love, wholeness, happiness, forfeit, choice, temptation, seduction, enchantment, lust, blindness, gamble, risk, fate, excitement, new pathway.

Offering: Water, green gemstones.

Contact: Apple is a tree of Venus and Friday is the day of Venus and of Freyja/Frigg. If you are able, go to Glastonbury Tor in Somerset, England, for this ritual. Standing outside the tower, look around you at the countryside which is strewn with hills. Imagine the hill is the center of the isle surrounded by water, as it was a long time ago. You are now on a magical isle. Only the hills will appear above the water as other isles. Of course not everyone can go to Glastonbury, so this ritual can also be conducted in front of an apple tree.

For the ritual you will need an apple and something to cut it in half *horizontally* to reveal the five pointed star, (or cut the apple in half before you leave and wipe the surface with lemon juice to prevent it from going brown placing in an airtight bag or container). Think of five things in your life that you wish to change. Contemplate on your wishes then eat the half apple. Work with the faery magic on a Friday or at the time of Samhain.

Appeal to the faeries for assistance in making your choice.

The Birch Wand
New Beginnings — Birth
Element: Water

The Birch Tree

In his poem *The Picture or The Lover's Resolution*, the poet Samuel Taylor Coleridge named the birch tree the *Most beautiful of forest trees, the Lady of the Woods*. The weeping branches of the silver birch droop gracefully and the dazzling silver white bark indeed makes this a beautiful tree to behold.

Witches use birch besoms for rituals and for flights. The brush is the birch twigs tied with willow strips and the handle is of ash wood.

And birch was and still is used to sweep out the Celtic old year at Samhain and is connected to the fertility festival Bealtaine.

The birch is a tree related to fertility and children and is a tree of new beginnings as indicated in Berkano the birch, is a rune of the Elder Futhark (see my book *The Spiritual Runes*).

Folklore

Although a tree of water, the birch tree is also associated with dryads.

The Scottish tree-dweller the Gille Dubh or Ghillie Dhu preferred the birch or birch thickets. He is a strange character with wild black hair and clothes woven of leaves and moss. He is reclusive but is also known to be compassionate, especially towards children.

Cradles and baby toys are often made with birch as it has protective qualities especially where children are concerned.

The traditional maypole, a fertility symbol, is made of birch and therefore has a great connection with the festival Bealtaine.

The Birch Wand in a Reading

With the birch tree a new beginning or birth is signified. As always with a new beginning it can cause smaller life changes, but more often than not these are more significant changes. This can be the birth of a baby, a marriage or new relationship, giving something a second chance, a project, career change or house move or anything that signifies the birth of something. Of course it has to grow and mature so will require nurturing.

The Gille Dubh is connected to children and protection. He will protect your new start (whatever that may be) while you nurture it. This will be hard but rewarding work.

The Birch Wand brings life-changes. As a fertile wand, new ideas abound and come into play which is not just the seed of something new but the beginning of something more substantial that will continue to grow.

Negative Reading: You have a problem letting go of old things even if they are not secure. Opportunities have arisen but are not being taken up perhaps from fear of failure. Perhaps you are not considering the positive aspects that your new life will bring, so will not give it a chance. You cannot change events but 'getting a grip' or 'moving on' is not always an easy thing to do. Throw yourself into a new project and do not look back. Becoming a part of it will be a lot easier than you had imagined.

Keywords: New beginnings, birth, protection, life changes, nurture, fertility, new ideas and projects.

Offering: Ribbons, nuts, water.

Contact: The birch is a tree of Venus and Friday is the day of the goddess Venus. When you need help with children or new beginnings ask the birch tree faeries for assistance.

The Gille Dubh can be found in Scotland at Gairloch on the northwest coast, and Loch Druing. Of course for most people, this will not be possible so head to the nearest birch tree or birch grove.

Have a cleansing bath to rid you of negativities. Water is a great purifier. Add salts and purifying oils to the bath water such as frankincense or lavender. Let the water drain away along with your negativities. If you only have a shower then you rub the oils mixed with the salt onto your body and then shower it away.

Try Friday for contact, Bealtaine or Samhain.

The Willow Wand
Inspiration, Healing, enchantment
Element: Water

The Willow Tree
The willow tree is the most beautiful of trees, especially the weeping willow, and is a sacred Druid tree. The old Irish name for it is Saille, though there are various spellings. The fronds reach down into the water and water is healing. The bark is intricate and has deep fissures. Put your hands on the trunk and feel the power.

Together with the ash and birch, willow is the third wood that makes up the witch's besom, its flexible branches or fronds tying the birch twigs together, while ash wood is the handle.

The willow loves water and it is near water you will more frequently find it growing, particularly near rivers. The willow is the sister tree of the alder, which although it appears here as a wand of fire, is also a tree of water. Willow is a tree of the moon and lunar magic. Magic wands sometimes come from the willow and in fact my own does.

Folklore
The willow tree is another tree of goddess, saint and faery, Brigid of the Tuatha Dé Dannan, and woman of the faery hills. Brigid is a fire goddess but is also linked with water and sacred wells. Imbolg her day of celebration, heralds the start of spring. Fertility begins to return to the land. Brigid is the patron of poets and a goddess of inspiration. She also has connections with

Excalibur and the Lady of the Lake, and is a shape-shifter and enchantress. Brigid is a midwife and healer and her healing waters are in the wells and streams, although she has connections with rivers and lakes too. Like many trees, the willow has associations with fertility of the land, but it is primarily a tree of inspiration especially of poets and musicians.

The water spirits of all kinds represent this tree. The merpeople have powers of healing and know much about healing herbs.

The Willow Wand in a Reading

The willow tree brings healing both physical and emotional. If you have been through a traumatic time, now is the time when healing will begin. Healing allows you to move forward and to begin again or resume your life. Willow leaves will protect you, so carry some with you at this time.

With Brigid comes inspiration. Small ideas will grow and mature into big ones. Soon the buds will appear. Now is the time to make plans and to sew the seeds of the future. Remember to nurture your ideas, think of yourself as a parent, the mother or father of them, and tend them. An exciting and productive time is predicted. Brigid will bring a new vitality to any relationship, and her magical waters will heal any rifts. If you are a writer, poet or storyteller, or have embarked on study of any kind, there is a creative and productive period ahead.

The merpeople will assist in the healing process and show you what you should do to help yourself.

The Willow Wand ensures that the future will be different. There has been a period of rest or dormancy, everything has been frozen in time and no progress has been made. Now is the time for all that to change. The buds of spring appear with new hope for the future. You can visualize the sun in the distance and will work your way towards it. Summer will come and with it comes better times. A new optimism takes hold of you, so use it to your best advantage.

Negative Reading: You are trapped in the past. You need to face up to and deal with those things that you would rather remain hidden often deep in your unconscious. It could be that you are wallowing in self pity and pessimism and the healing process cannot break through the barrier you have erected. Lower the barriers and so allow yourself to heal. You cannot change the past but you can influence the future. Listen to the inner you as it has something significant to say. Use your intuition. You will be surprised to discover that things could be very different for you, were you to step out from the prison you have created for yourself. Even if you believe others put you there, only you are keeping you there.

Keywords: Inspiration, healing, lunar magic, fertility, spring, new life, poets and musicians, study, creativity, productiveness, new hope, optimism, protection.

Offering: Ribbons, candles, spring water, primroses, mugwort.

Contact: During the New Moon and up until the Full Moon is the time for contact with Brigid and this tree, but also on the day of the moon, Monday. Imbolg is the time to think about where your future is going and to formulate plans. Collect leaves for protection thanking the willow for them and asking for help before making your wishes. Stand under the weeping willow fronds and feel its protection.

Find a willow by a river or lake to appeal to the merpeople for help, especially in emotional matters.

The Hazel Wand
Knowledge, Wisdom, Inspiration
Element: Water

The Hazel Tree

The hazel tree was sacred to the Druids, and lies at the heart of the Otherworld. The tree is occasionally to be found near holy wells. The hazel resembles a shrub more than a tree, but it does appear occasionally with a single trunk and it thrives in damp places. The fruit of the hazel is known by all, and its pliable wood has many uses including walking sticks, staffs, and hoops. Rods of hazel are used to dowse for water. A Y-shaped branch is cut and used to make natural handles. When the point twitches, water, energy or minerals can be found.

Folklore

The hazel tree grows near to Connla's Well (this is a second Connla of Celtic mythology), which lies under the sea in the *Land of Youth*. The fruit and blossom of wisdom, knowledge and inspiration, fall into the well causing a flow of purple onto the water. Salmon chew on the fruit and take on the color which gives them speckles. The well and the water in it, the salmon and the hazel, all together make a magical combination. The faery goddess Sinann, daughter of Lir the great sea god, went to the well and it appears was either not permitted to do so, or omitted to perform certain ceremony, and the angry water washed her away towards the ocean. Her body came to rest on the shore of a river, which from thence on was named the Shannon, after her. The Shannon

River lies in Ireland.

Nine hazel trees also grow close to the magical well of wisdom called Segais. Again the hazel fruit falls into the water and is eaten by the salmon. This time it is Boann, meaning 'White Cow' the wife of Nechtan (although some sources give other names), who was the lover of the Dagda with whom she had a son. Her husband was guardian of the well. In this case Boann did not follow the protocol of the well, and walked around it widdershins (counter clockwise). Like Sinann she was swept away by a surge of water losing or injuring an arm, a leg and an eye, and eventually her life. The resulting river, the Boyne, was named after her. The River Boyne runs close to a cluster of sidhe mounds in Ireland, including Newgrange.

There are two tree spirits attached to guarding the hazel tree in England, Melsh Dick and Churnmilk Peg of Yorkshire.

The hazel appears in many superstitions regarding divining, you throw two nuts into the fire if you are trying to choose between lovers. The first one to crack is the true one. You can also throw two nuts in the fire to represent you and your lover, if they burn long and slow together, you will be happy. If one nut jumps apart from the other, you will not.

The Hazel Wand in a Reading

The hazel tree is a magical tree; it provides us with knowledge, wisdom, and inspiration. In a reading the hazel tree shows you that you have the power within and on which to work. Your knowledge will grow with the inspiration you have already been gifted. Wisdom usually comes with age and experience, yet you have the seeds of this wisdom ripening within and others will be surprised at how wise you can already be.

Sinann and Boann teach you that knowledge, wisdom, and inspiration can not be instantly won. Certainly it appears that with the magical well of wisdom, certain ritual must be performed. Often it is a teacher who provides you with the food of wisdom, as indicated by the salmon. The salmon is both the teacher and the food of knowledge and wisdom. You need to decide from whom or from where the fount of wisdom comes and how you can go about learning from it. It should be obvious to you. If not then your intuition is trying to tell you something. Try a contact method below to ask for this to reveal itself to you.

Melsh Dick and Churnmilk Peg as guardians will provide protection just as they protect the hazel tree.

The Hazel Wand in a reading shows that you have the powers of communication and persuasion. You are struck with the gift of wisdom and inspiration. New ideas spring forth, and you may well be guided by someone wiser than yourself, so that this wisdom and knowledge can grow. Use this wisely. You have a chance to improve yourself and if you ignore this chance you might one day regret it.

Negative Reading: You have not shown wisdom and without thinking you have jumped in with both feet. Take a step back and rethink your strategy. Perhaps you are impulsive and over excited, or it could be that you have a fear of learning, wrongly thinking you are not clever enough. You do have the power within you to move forward and to learn new skills, it is never too late. Do not reject good advice.

Keywords: Knowledge, wisdom, inspiration, power within, teacher or mentor, good advice, communication, persuasion, guidance, divination, protection.

Offering: Gemstones, ribbons, flowers.

Contact: The hazel is a tree of Mercury, so contact day is Wednesday. The Autumn Equinox is a time of the second harvest and autumn a time when the hazel nuts are ripe. If you find a well with a hazel tree nearby then walk around the well deosil (clockwise) three times and leave an offering. Ask for the gift of wisdom, but do not demand it as your right. If you get the chance, visit the faery mounds of Ireland particularly those in the Boyne valley. Go to the River Boyne or the River Shannon and throw a gift of a gemstone into the river and take some inspiration from the water. Otherwise go and visit any holy well or river or directly to the hazel tree. Eat hazelnuts as part of the ritual if possible from the tree itself.

Fire and the Salamanders

The Wands of Fire, Rowan, Alder, Holly and Yew, deal with the unconscious and intuition, but also energy, creativity, confidence, vision, rebirth and regeneration. Fire is the torch of light in darkness, warmth in the winter, and provides heat for cooking. However, fire is not easy to control. Too much fire can lead to aggression, uncontrollability and irresponsibility.

Fire people are those born under the signs of Aries, Leo and Sagittarius.

Salamanders are an elemental lizard or spirit of fire and materialize from the flames. They are powerful creatures and can vary in size depending on the fire from which they materialize. Keeping your fire under control is paramount to keeping the salamander calm as this creature can be mischievous or even dangerous if treated without respect. All fires have salamanders so you do not have to travel far to have contact with them.

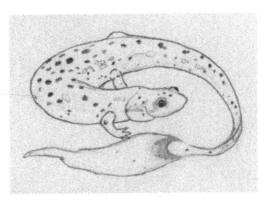

Keywords: Intuition, unconscious, creativity, torch, comfort, energy, action, vision, confidence, power, psychic abilities, willpower, strength, protection, transformation, rebirth and regeneration.

Color: Red

The Rowan Wand
Protection, Psychic Power, Personal Power
Element: Fire

The Rowan Tree
The rowan tree is also called the Mountain Ash even though it is not a member of the ash family and is a favorite tree of the Scottish highlands. The rowan has clusters of fragrant creamy-white blossom in spring and lovely red berries in the autumn, though they never last long as they are a huge attraction for the birds. The berries are edible but taste rather bitter and are more often used in jams. The rowan is one of autumn's most colorful trees with pink, gold and scarlet leaves. As it is a strong wood, over the centuries, rowan has been used to make spinning wheels, spindles and walking sticks.

Although many trees have protective qualities, the rowan tree is perhaps the most protective of all and is foremost in protection against negative influences. At the stalk end of the berries you will see a tiny five pointed star or pentagram, a magical and ancient symbol of protection. The rowan has protected homes for centuries.

Folklore
The dragon is the rowan tree guardian. It appears frequently in Celtic myth often depicted as a serpent type creature or worm. When the dragon or worm swallows its own tale it symbolizes immortality, which is a rowan tree feature. Dragons or worms can be guardians, particularly of the Otherworld.

The Salamander is also guardian of fire and a creative force.

The rowan is yet another tree sacred to Brigid of the Tuatha Dé Danann patron of crafts and spinning, as spinning wheels were once made from rowan wood. Her fiery arrows are also said to have been made from rowan wood.

In the following tale as with all mythology there are various spellings of the names of the characters involved. Deep in the Forest of Dooras there was a Fomorian one-eyed giant, protector of the rowan or quicken tree of immortality, called Searbhan the Surly One. He guarded the tree for the faery tribe of Tuatha Dé Danann. The tree had grown from a berry which came from faeryland having been accidentally dropped by the faery folk. It was indeed a magical tree. A runaway couple Diarmuid and Grainne came upon the tree while being pursued by Fionn who was Grainne's spurned husband to be. Grainne requested berries from the tree which were said to taste as sweet as honey. After a battle, Searbhan was slain by Diarmuid with three strikes of his own iron club. Diarmuid was then able to obtain the berries for his love, Grainne.

The Rowan Wand in a Reading

The rowan tree offers you magical protection. This protection allows you to be more creative and outgoing. You can confidently move forward with projects. If you are afraid how others will view your actions, do not be, as all will come good. Any initial objection will soon be overcome. You are capable of a quiet and resilient strength, so use it to your advantage.

Personal power is symbolized by the dragon and salamander. The dragon is guardian spirit and creative force, which along with the salamander adds a fiery aspect to events. This fiery aspect is within you at this time; use it in making your views known on particular endeavors connected to you. You do not need to defend these views or ideas, so hold back and simply explain your reasons in a simple fashion. These reasons will have to be accepted as your strength and determination will show through. This fiery aspect can also be used for creative purposes.

The tale of the pursuit of Diarmuid and Grainne show that with the killing of the indestructible Searbhan, no one is invincible or nothing impossible. If you want something then you only have to try harder to get it. Losing control is what can cause you to be defeated, so even though your natural defensive shield is in place, keep calm and focused.

Psychic power is in abundance with Brigid and the Tuatha Dé Danann providing your intuition with a well needed boost of energy. Use this to make decisions and to lead you along life's new pathway. Regenerative forces abound, so perhaps a new project, house move, or career change is in the offing.

The Rowan Wand is indeed a powerfully magical one. Life will take a new turn and you will feel more in control than you have for a long while. Nurture this and point it in the right direction. Let a creative mind run free but keep focused on goals and try not to become too distracted. The Rowan Wand is related to the other three fire wands, though the rowan is more a preparation for the new phase ahead, rather than the phase itself.

Negative Reading: You are hiding behind your inner dragon perhaps from fear. You are afraid to spread your wings, to learn new things and tap into your personal and psychic power. This power is a magical power and you are afraid it will get out of control, so have your dragon so tamed it can no longer fly and expressive itself in a creative and imaginative way. Try not to be so rational.

There is an opposing view with this dragon. Another reason for hiding behind your inner dragon and in this case the salamander too, is that you have let it get out of control so it is wild and unmanageable, as fire itself can indeed become uncontrollable if not contained. Yet it can be tamed without subjugating it entirely. By taming your inner dragon to work with you rather than against, you will feel more protected and can use your creative nature in a more constructive way, finishing tasks.

With both these problems a balance needs to be struck between letting creative expression have its freedom and not letting it get so out of hand that you are no longer in control, but it controls you. Keep focused.

Keywords: Protection, psychic power, personal power, creativity, resilience, strength, intuition, energy, regeneration, new projects.

Offering: Red ribbons, gemstones, incense, candles.

Contact: Rowan is a tree of the sun. Contact is best on a Sunday, and during fire and solar festivals which are any of the Celtic Wheel of the Year festivals as shown at the end of this book. The solar festivals are the seasonal changes of the solstices and equinoxes, and the fire festivals are the other four cross quarter days. However, as the rowan is a tree of Brigid and Imbolg, this cross-quarter fire festival is perhaps the best along with Bealtaine and the Summer Solstice.

Request from Diarmuid and Grainne the determination to succeed. The Tuatha dé Dannan can be called upon to assist you in increasing psychic awareness.

Leave an offering, burn a candle and some incense, and request protection, psychic or personal power.

If you wish to repel negative influences, visit a rowan tree and take a twig or two after leaving your offering (a windfall is best), but however you obtain them then ask permission first and express your gratitude. Carry the rowan twigs with you wherever you go, tied with red thread or ribbon. This will not only protect you but will also increase your psychic and personal power.

The Holly Wand
Recharging, Hope, Future Regeneration
Element: Fire

The Holly Tree
The holly tree needs no introduction as it is recognizable to all. Holly is the tree we love to have in our homes at Yuletide to celebrate the return of the light. Its dark green shiny leaves and bright red berries symbolize fertility within the barren winter, not the least that it cheers us with its beauty and color. Holly brings eternal hope, growth and renewal.

The holly is another protective tree and was said to repel magic, to drain opponents of their strength and protect homes from lightening. Only the female tree produces the cheerful red berries though both the male and female tree produce fragrant white blossom in early summer. At Yuletide the holly is coupled with the ivy. Strangely though, the berried holly is known as the 'king' and the ivy the 'queen'.

Folklore
The holly is a tree of Danu who is the mother of the Tuatha Dé Danann. She is goddess and faery queen. The Danube is said to have been named after her. Not much is known about her but she is the goddess of the faery people and the fertile land. She is also sometimes said to be the mother of the Dagda whom she begot with the oak tree *Bile* after watering it.

The unicorn is associated with the holly tree and is arguably the most magical of animals. Usually white with the legs and head of a horse — although it also appears in other guises — it has a spiraled magical horn in the middle of its forehead. The flaming Celtic spear is said to have been named after this magical horn. The unicorn symbolizes purity, strength and goodness. Its horn has healing properties for the body and the heart and also symbolizes sexual energy.

The holly tree appears in Celtic mythology. The Holly King is a powerful giant figure of nature wearing holly foliage. He rules the half year from the Summer Solstice until the Winter Solstice (Yule), taking over the role from his twin brother the defeated Oak King. He is the king of darkness and the waning year. The Holly and Oak Kings are speculated to have been the Green Knight (the holly) and Sir Gawain (the oak) of Arthurian legend. They take turns in beheading each other but remain magically alive.

The Holly Wand in a Reading

The holly tree celebrates the return of the light and with it you will begin to recharge your personal battery. It has been a time of rest or even dormancy when nothing much has happened and everything appears to be on hold. It could be that there has been a time of respite, time taken out of work perhaps as a sabbatical, because of recent childbirth, or through illness. You have hope for the future even if you have not yet formed plans, or if you have, are not yet able to put them into practice. Now is the time to gradually recharge ready for the metaphorical or actual spring. And spring brings promise. Build up your energy by slowly beginning to work at the things you wish to do perhaps in two or three months time from now.

Danu mother of the faery race will nurture you through the coming weeks while you gradually build energy for the forth-coming changes in your life.

If you have been ill, depressed, suffering pain of the heart, or something else has caused a freeze in your situation, the unicorn provides healing and informs you it is time to move on with your life.

The Holly King is at the end of his rule and with him goes the bleakness and the darkness of winter. The light becomes brighter and new growth appears.

The Holly Wand indicates forthcoming changes, gradual renewal and regeneration. Events have remained static and even if you have wished to move forward or take the next step you have been unable to do so. The time is coming when this will be possible. Small changes will begin to appear and this will build into something more significant. Watch out for the signs of this as they will provide you with hope and optimism. Do not worry about the future as nothing will harm you now. You are protected and negative influences in your life will be repelled. The Holly Wand is related to the other three fire wands, though the holly is perhaps the prophecy of an eventual new phase of life.

Negative Reading: You have no hope as you have let yourself become too overpowered by events. You have lost the will to move forward. Perhaps you feel as if you have had one blow after another. However, with a little effort things can be different. You are not stuck in this cycle as everything moves on. Reluctant as you are to change your situation from fear of the future and from not having faith in yourself, an effort still has to be made. Baby steps at first will gradually build up your confidence and then you will be able to see the forthcoming light in your life, which is far from over.

Keywords: Recharging, hope, future regeneration, fertility, light in the darkness, growth, goodness, protection, strength, optimism, repelling of negativity.

Offering: Leave red and green ribbon to symbolize growth and energy. Burn a candle to symbolize the burning of the holly and the end of a winter period.

Contact: Holly is a tree of Saturn and Saturday is the day of Saturn. The Winter Solstice is an ideal time for contact before the winter starts to wane and the oak takes over, otherwise the Summer Solstice when the summer starts waning and the holly takes over from the oak. At other times of year, the New Moon is appropriate to new growth. Contact on Saturday although occasionally the holly is associated with fiery Mars whose day is Tuesday.

Request assistance from Danu in encouraging new growth.

The Alder Wand
Regeneration, Resurrection, Leadership
Element: Fire equal with Water

The Alder Tree

The alder is a tree of fire but also of water and is another sacred tree as most are in this oracle. Alder is neither the tallest nor longest lived of trees. Not easily consumed by fire its slow burning wood makes good charcoal. It has the power of fire and therefore regeneration, and is associated with the early sun of spring.

The alder tree is fire but is equally a tree of water, and as this is an indication of fiery emotion. The alder grows in damp places and often close to water. The alder wood is water resistant and was often used for building bridges, jetties and pumps or anything that has contact with water. However, it did and does have many other uses, such as spinning wheels, clogs, bowls and spoons.

Folklore

The alder is a faery tree, and an entrance or portal to the Otherworld is through a doorway in its trunk. The faeries of this tree might occasionally take the form of birds when leaving it, especially that of the raven.

Bran, whose name means 'Raven', is the god associated with the alder and is a giant. He was the son of the sea god *Lyr* and the grandson of the sun god *Belenos*. He was a leader in battle and held twigs of alder.

The phoenix is associated with resurrection and is a sun symbol and is periodically consumed by fire only to rise again from the ashes.

Through Bran, the raven is linked to the alder. Ravens are sometimes depicted as wise. Two ravens accompanied the Norse god Odin, one was called *Hugin* (thought) and the other *Munin* (memory), connecting it with the conscious and unconscious self. The raven is associated with light, prophecy and wisdom, but above all it symbolizes the sun.

The Alder Wand in a Reading

The alder tree combines its fiery aspects with emotional water influences. At this time you have resilience. If you have drawn the Holly Wand previous to the alder, then this is the next stage for you. The spring is nigh and regeneration is at hand. New relationships, or more likely the resurrection of old ones perhaps of love, are possible at this time. You are a natural leader and can now take control again.

The alder tree faeries and creatures are of the darker kind, especially the salamander. They represent your unconscious but open the doorway for you to a brighter world. You will step into this world and all will be different.

The phoenix helps you rise again from the ashes of your previous life. A new career is perhaps in the offing. You are capable of great leadership so use those skills to help you and others. The raven symbolizes the rising sun. Things are beginning to warm up for you. You are capable of achieving balance as your enthusiasm and newly found energy rise to great heights.

The Alder Wand promises a new creative you, filled with determination and zeal. You are regenerated and entering a better phase in your life. You will lead the way forward with confidence. Enjoy the moment, but remember to consider the future while battling with your new life. The Alder Wand is related to the other three fire wands though it signifies more of a period of regeneration, while the Yew Wand signifies rebirth.

Negative Reading: Your emotions are too high, try to keep them under control or it can lead to impetuousness in your enthusiasm. You could be in the throws of a relationship, generally at the start, in which sex is energetic, fiery, and consumes you. This is a time when throwing water on the situation can calm it down. Go to a body of water, preferably a lake and breathe in the tranquility. Try to be calm and consider what you are doing. Perhaps there is a desperation involved in this.

As a natural leader your enthusiasm can be getting everyone else down. Not everyone can keep up with you and it is unreasonable to expect them to. Try not to be so impulsive and calmly go about your business. Energetic enthusiasm is fine, as long as the power does not consume you, and blind you to what you are doing. You should use this time of regeneration to help you move forward in a more controlled way.

Be careful not to battle with all who are only trying to help you.

Keywords: Regeneration, resurrection, leadership, sun, light, spring, water, prophecy, transformation, balance, enthusiasm, impetuosity.

Offering: Water, red gemstones, particularly garnet or ruby, light candles.

Contact: The alder is a tree of Venus, but also of a water sign, perhaps Pisces. The alder is also associated with fiery Mars and the warming Sun. The Spring Equinox is a good time of year for contact. Otherwise Sunday, Tuesday, and Friday, and the time of Pisces which is from February 19th – March 21st.

Take some alder twigs from around the tree and hold them while you make your wish. You can later use them to make a magic pen as they make good charcoal. Burn the end of the twig for a while until it is black enough to write with. When it wears down, burn it some more. Use the pen to write messages and bury them at the tree's base or burn them.

The New Moon time is a three days span of darkness but with it comes the gradual moonlight. Contact during the New Moon is a good time for connection with the alder spirits.

The Yew Wand
Death and Rebirth
Element: Fire

The Yew Tree

Though not a tall tree, the yew is a strong and has an extremely long life. The oldest yew in Europe (Scotland) is though to be 3,000 years old. All of its parts are poisonous to humans, although deer love to feed off it. Yew is the tree of immortality as it symbolizes death and rebirth. When a yew dies, new ones grow from branches that touch the ground and grow into independent trees around the old trunk. The yew has the power of renewal as new grows from the old. This beautiful evergreen tree was sometimes called the tree of death as it is grown in graveyards (or it could even be that graveyards were formed where there were yew trees). A strong argument exists that the yew tree is the World Tree and not the ash tree. As such there is a link with elves and giants, and the animals associated with Yggdrasil. Yew wood was traditionally used for longbows. The fire within is holy, purifying and renewing. The yew signifies rebirth on a higher level and is protective.

Folklore

In the Celtic tale of the wooing of Etain, it is told of how a Druid was asked by Eochaid to find his missing wife (Etain). The Druid, by writing Oghams on four wands of yew, found her living with Midir in the faery mound or sidhe of the Bri Leith. Etain had been married to Midir in her former life, but she was killed by his first wife who had changed her into a purple fly. In trying to escape she had eventually fallen into a drinking cup and was swallowed by the chieftain's wife Etar. The wife of Etar had then fallen pregnant and in due time gave birth once more to Etain, who reborn lived her life again not knowing anything of her previous identity.

The forest stag is associated with Yggdrasil and feeds off the bark off the yew as indeed deer love to feed off it. Its great antlers symbolize fire. It shows itself when the Otherworld is close. The stag represents the life force or spiritual energy within which lives with us and withdraws after death. This energy can heal us and unify our mind, body and spirit.

The Yew Wand in a Reading

The Yew tree symbolizes rebirth. This also means the death of something. However, where there is death there is also new life. All old things must die for the new ones to begin. Look at what in your past is affecting the here and now and try to resolve it. Clean out what is old and unnecessary ready for the new phase.

The transition could be a spiritual or personal one. You are about to cross over from the darkness into the welcoming light. If things are not going so well it could be that they will improve soon. Prepare for this, renewal is just around the corner.

Etain was reborn forgetting her old life. Although you will not forget your old life it is time to put it behind you so that you can move forward with a completely new start. All sorts of adventures befell Etain in her new life, and the same will happen with you no matter what your age.

The stag is a forest solar animal, his antlers representing sunrays and fire. He brings you protection and mediation between heaven and earth. This is a spiritual message between you and the Otherworld. The stag is there at the rebirth providing a vital recharge of spiritual energy, which helps in the healing process and provides balance and a better understanding between the conscious and unconscious.

The Yew Wand offers protection, reliability, and a steadfast quiet strength. It will provide protection during the transitional stage or the passing from one stage of life to the next. The changes will bring a new light and a new existence. The Yew Wand is related to the other three fire wands, though the yew is complete rebirth, rather than regeneration or preparation of your new phase of life.

Negative Reading: You are finding it difficult to put the past behind you so that you can fully move forward to your new future. You have a fear that the past will repeat itself and although you want to move on, in a way, past traumas provide security. In that misplaced feeling of security you have become too accustomed to your lot, while the future brings uncertainty and you doubt you can survive. The unconscious has hidden traumas too, which need bringing forth and healing. If something has ended that you have a problem dealing with, take heart. Although you cannot bring something dead back to life, you can begin again and this will bring you new joys. The yew tree stag can help you with this.

It really is time for your new life. Somewhere out there it awaits you, so embrace it and all will be well.

Keywords: Death and rebirth, immortality, renewal, purifying, protection, transition, quiet strength, spiritual energy, mediation.

Offering: Incense, gemstones particularly the white or clear ones.

Contact: The yew falls under the influence of Saturn, so Saturday is the day for contact. Other times are the New Moon, Samhain (the Celtic New Year), and Bealtaine for fertility, and Imbolg or the Spring Equinox for new life. Yew trees can be found in church yards and cemeteries if you have a problem locating one.

Ask the stag to mediate between you and the Otherworld in asking for assistance.

The Elementals Wand
Positive
Elementals: Gnomes, Sylphs, Undines (Earth, Air, Water)

The Elementals Wand which combines the qualities of *earth, air and water*, can change a wand's meaning to a positive one. (See Diagram 1, 2 and 3 for instructions on spreads).

If a wand has an accompanying Elemental Wand then the meaning becomes either positive or its positive qualities are enhanced. When you read that particular wand then you should change any negative aspects to positive or the more positive aspects will be even greater.

The elementals of air bring a calm balance to events, along with thought and wisdom. Earth elementals deal with practical troubles, and water elementals emotional responsibility. The Elementals Wand lacks a fiery passion and extra energy, but it indicates we are acting rationally and not letting the past or passion affect our decisions and lives.

The Salamander Wand
Negative
Elemental: Salamander (Fire)

The Salamander Wand which contains the quality of *fire*, can change a wand's meaning to a negative one. (See Diagram 1, 2 and 3 for instructions on spreads).

You will find a negative meaning with each wand or Portal which should be read *after* you read the general meanings (as you still need to know all about that wand), but it is the negative reading that applies.

The Salamander Wand represents fire and as such reveals the unconscious mind of the subject is affecting the meaning. We all hide away things in the unconscious, things we wish to forget, and this frequently comes back to cause a blockage in our lives. It also represents too much fire connected to the particular problem being addressed, which causes aggression, uncontrollability or irresponsibility.

The Elementals or Salamander Wand usually affects the wand which comes immediately after it and to save confusion should be placed across that wand.

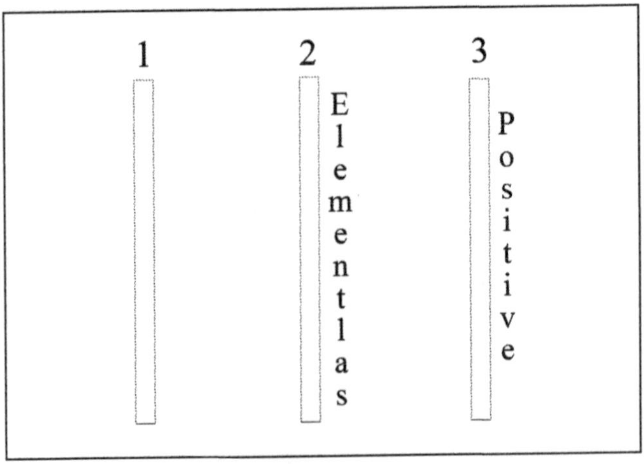

Diagram 1

If the Elementals Wand or Salamander Wand appears at the end of the row choose another wand and cross it.

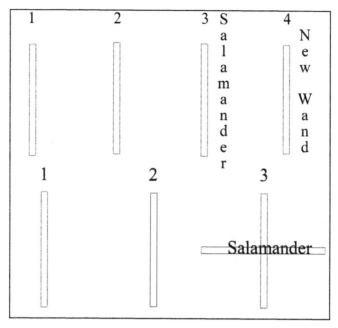

Diagram 2

In a row of only two wands, the wand that lies along side whether it comes before or after the Elementals Wand or Salamander Wand becomes positive or negative.

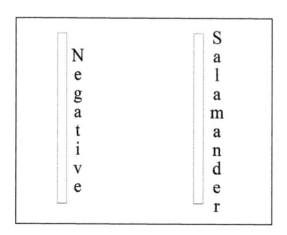

Diagram 3

Making the Faery Caille

To make your oracle from wands of wood, then you need to go out to walk in the forest, in parks, or even in your neighborhood or the gardens of friends, in fact anywhere there are trees to be found.

The most ideal way to find your wands is to look for the specific trees that match each one. Of course this will only be possible if every species grows where you live.

What I did was to collect the wands from those trees that I could find in my area, others were gathered gradually from places I traveled to, and in the meantime the rest I made from one of my favorite trees, the willow.

The added benefit from finding the correct woods is that you learn to identify trees and their positions, which is wonderful for when you wish to make contact with the faeries in the future. If it is just impossible to find all the trees varieties, then just choose one kind of wood. Beech and yew were known to have been used for the Ogham so both are suitable woods. Alternatively, any portal tree of oak, ash and hawthorn, or indeed any tree with which you have an affinity, as I have with the willow, will be suitable.

You will find that wood cannot be easily written on even if you shave away a little bark. Carving is the best way and you can buy a carving tool (widely available) or pyrograph to burn the symbols onto the wood and which are available from craft shops.

You can leave or scrape away bark, and polish, varnish or wax your wood if you desire. I prefer to leave mine natural with the bark intact to allow the powers of the wood to be easily released. However, wood is porous and some barks can flake, though I have not yet had that problem.

Alternatively, some people use ice lolly sticks, or something similar, which can be written on, or any strips of wood such as those used to mark planting.

When you collect the wands, be sure to label them with the

name of the tree as you will not remember which is which later.

You can bless and cleanse your wands by passing them through Frankincense smoke. Concentrate on the meaning of each one as you do so. This will help you with the connection. Other ways of blessing and empowering are explained in my book, *The Spiritual Runes,* and this method can also be used for the Faery Caille.

If you wish you can use a cloth to cast or place your wands upon. The colors I would suggest for your cloth are white, green, silver, purple or gold.

Making Cards

You can buy sheets of card either white or colored and already sectioned off in stationery shops. Mark each one with a symbol of a wand, and the name if you desire. However, it is easier to learn the symbols if you leave the name off.

Spreads and Readings

How to use Wands and Cards

With wood wands you can either throw them directly onto grass, or onto your cloth. You then choose one at a time the appropriate amount for the particular reading laying them out as indicated.

With card wands you should shuffle them and either fan them out and choose one at a time, or cut them the appropriate amount of times, replacing the cut cards at the bottom of the pile and choosing the card that is now on top of the pack. Another way is to cut several piles at one time (three for the Faery Queen Spread, five for the Spindle Spread and so forth), and then take the top card from each pile.

Before throwing or choosing the wands, think about the question you wish to ask or problem you wish to solve, and ask for the appropriate help as indicated by each reading.

I will talk about 'wands' in each reading, and this applies to both wood wands and card wands.

The Faery Queen Spread (Three Wands)

A Faery Queen reading works better if you ask about only one aspect of a situation, for situations have many aspects. It pins down causes and effects of the particular problem and gives you the opportunity to redirect the future.

With this reading the three wands drawn or chosen, represent the past, present and possible future.

The first wand shows you what in the past has caused the problem. The second wand shows you what in the present is preventing the problem from being resolved. The third wand can show you what the possible outcome of this problem will be, or if it will remain unresolved. Knowing what it is that caused and is continuing to keep this problem active, can help you in working it out.

Thinking of what the problem is and asking the faery queens to show you the way, throw all of your wood wands onto grass or your cloth and choose three as described above laying them down side by side. Alternatively, and if you are using cards, choose three card wands.

The first wand represents the past, the second the present and the third the future. You should read them from left to right.

The Spindle Spread

The Spindle Spread is an extension of the Faery Queen Spread as both are associated with the Spindle Wand. In this reading choose five wands one at a time as described above and then lay them out as indicated by the diagram.

The bottom wand represents the past. The middle wands reading from left to right represent the time just before the present, the present time, and the near future. The top wand represents the future.

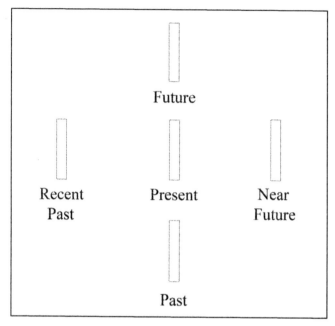

The Spindle Spread

The Elemental Spread

An Elemental reading consists of eight wands. These are chosen and then arranged in the order chosen and in the following way (see diagram).

The first two wands are Earth and the second two wands are Water. Earth needs water and water provides nourishment to help growth. When reading, the Water Wands should complement the Earth Wands and can be read in relation to them (see sample reading).

The third two wands are Fire and the fourth two wands are Air. Air fans fire, gives it more power and keeps it alive. When reading, the Air Wands should complement the Fire Wands and can be read in relation to them (see sample reading).

The first wand of each couple represents the state of affairs, and the second wand provides advice.

Earth shows you the practical considerations of the state of affairs.
Water shows you the emotional considerations.
Fire shows you the strength and foresight aspects.
Air shows you the knowledge and thought aspects.

If you have chosen the Elementals Wand then it enhances the accompanying wand's positive qualities (in this case another wand in not chosen). If you have chosen the Salamander Wand, then you should use the negative reading for the accompanying wand. If both are chosen together as a pair, then disregard them and choose two more wands to replace them.

	State of Affairs	Advice
Earth		
Water		
Fire		
Air		

The Elementals Spread

Sample Elemental Reading
Here is a brief sample reading to show how this particular spread

works. The problem highlighted in this reading, concerns a job change. Freda is a single mum with two young teenage children and feels her job is not only unchallenging but she is unhappy with the work she is doing. She is now *thinking* of seeking new employment and although she really feels this is her only option and in fact welcomes the idea, she is a little wary and wants oracular advice on the matter, even though her father is supportive of the idea. Her main concern is leaving her colleagues as she has a good rapport with them and is reluctant to lose this as she might not have that in a new position. Her closest friend thinks she is crazy to leave all the security she has in her present position, and there is conflict between them concerning this, as the friend has a dominant personality.

Earth Couplet
The Oak Portal/*State of Affairs*
The Oak Portal advises that home life must be a stable and firm base established before moving on. If Freda has established this then perhaps it is time to move forward on life's pathway. Freda assures me her home life is stable and she feels she is ready for new challenges. The Oak Portal assures her that she will have the strength and the dryads and oakmen the protection to succeed, but she must protect what is hers and accept advice from those wiser. Freda has already had good advice from her father which reflects the need to ensure a good and secure new position, before leaving her present one. Success and prosperity is assured, if all these matters have been carefully considered. Brigid rewards hard work and as Freda is a hard worker a reward is certain. The Dagda will help her overcome any difficulties and opposition.

The Yew Wand/*Advice*
The Yew Wand advises that the birth of something is imminent, but for the birth something else must die. The death of

something not only relates to the old employment, but also to move forward, Freda will have to leave behind that special rapport she has with her old colleagues. As with Etain, Freda can look forward to new adventures in her next job and she will have the spiritual strength as well as the inner strength to form new relationships. The yew's fire aspect will provide the extra strength of character to achieve what she sets out to do. Freda does not have to lose contact with any real friends she has made in her present position. She can walk into the light to enjoy her new experiences.

Water Couplet
The Holly Wand/*State of Affairs*

The Holly Wand very much reflects the first two wands. Emotionally Freda had been rather down if not depressed because of her present job, and this is affecting her general mood and hence her relationship with her children. Changing her job could take time and Danu and the unicorn are at hand to help her in the healing process. She can look forward to her new future and will have time to prepare for the new venture. The Holly King demise ensures the end of the bleakness that has surrounded her. The fiery aspects of this wand will help in the recharging of Freda's personal batteries. She can look forward to regeneration with hope and renewed optimism.

The Cherry Wand/*Advice*

The Cherry Wand brings inner strength and balance. Freda can deal with opposition to her forthcoming plans with inner calmness. Her strong intuition will help her in tackling the opposition from her closest friend without losing face, but maintaining their previously good relationship. Perhaps compromises are necessary such as listening or taking on board of some the advice from the friend, but only that which Freda feels will not affect her decision. The Vilas of air are there to help in the compromises. By not giving in to these outer powerful influences, Freda will become an emotionally stronger and more confident person.

With the emotional strength assured the practical aspects of future plans will fall into place and Freda will remain resolute and focused.

Fire Couplet
The Blackthorn Wand/*State of Affairs*
Although the outlook is good, the blackthorn indicates it will not be a totally smooth ride for Freda. She has opposition to her plans. As the Blackthorn Wand says, someone is literally being a thorn in her side, which is possibly her friend as strife does exist between them. Freda is going through difficulties at work and in her personal life. Her strong intuition is suggesting to her that changes need to be made. The Faery Godmother is looking after her ensuring that she will go to the ball. The Lunantishee add protection helping to build a thorny hedge of defense around her. Negative energy will bounce off Freda and her fiery determination will win through. It is time for change and soon spring will arrive for her.

The Willow Wand/*Advice*
The Willow Wand portends an exciting time ahead. But the suggestion she needs healing shows Freda she has been emotionally ill. Carrying willow leaves around with her will help in the healing process and if it is winter time then a twig or piece of frond can also be carried. Any strife causing her anguish at this time will eventually improve. The water aspects of this wand will help to heal the rifts between Freda and her friend. The Willow Wand also reflects the Blackthorn in that better times are coming and Freda should hold onto this.

Air Couplet
The Spindle Wand (*accompanied by the* Salamander Wand)/*State of Affairs*

The Spindle Wand has the Salamander Wand to accompany it. This means the Spindle Wand's negative meaning should be read. Freda still has a problem that has not been fully addressed which is moving away from the good relationship she currently has with her colleagues. Freda is aware this should not hold her back and yet it is. Her reluctance to move onto her new pathway in life because of this is one of the causes of her depression and unhappiness. She is stuck in a rut and is not progressing. Change will not happen by itself, we have to work hard to make it happen. Making firm plans and deciding exactly what step to take to instigate these changes will help Freda feel more in control of the situation. Even though she is worried she may regret making changes, in the future she is likely to wish she had done something sooner and not wasted so much time, but she should not dwell on this. As long as the plans are carefully thought out, then her decision to make changes will never be regretted. This could be a time to call on her wise father for support.

At this point general advice would be for Freda to have a cleansing bath as indicated in the oracle to assist in the ridding of negativities, to rid her of her unconstructive thoughts, and to help her with her fresh start.

Good planning and forethought will help her to promote creative and fiery energy.

Faery Ring Spread
Seven wands are chosen and placed in a circle clockwise beginning at the top (see diagram).

1

7   2

6   3

5   4

Faery Ring Spread

1. The top or first wand indicates the problem.
2. The second wand shows you what is obvious about the problem.
3. The third wand reveals what is hidden.
4. The fourth wand shows you what in the past has affected this problem.
5. The fifth wand shows you any outside influences that may be contributing.
6. The sixth provides advice.
7. The seventh wand shows you what the likely outcome of this problem will be.

If you draw a Salamander or Elementals Wand then draw another wand and place it crosswise on top. The new wand drawn will take on either the positive or negative meaning.

Quick Wand Reference

Wand	Meaning
Oak (*Portal*)	*Strength, stability, and success through hard work are assured. You are protected.* (Dryads, Oakmen, Brigid)
Ash (*Portal*)	*You have blockages but healing is in sight. Look within for answers and use your intuition. Your strength grows stronger and you are freer.* (Elves, Dwarfs, Frost and Fire Giants, Meliae)
Hawthorn (*Portal*)	*Good luck with protection is yours. This is a fertile time for you. Beware of negative influences.* (All Faeries)
Elm (*Earth*)	*Metamorphosis is indicated. The caterpillar transforms into a butterfly. A more fulfilling life pathway is ahead.* (Elves)
Elder (*Earth*)	*Challenges at the present time with a prosperous time ahead. Share your abundance, but do not let others take advantage.* (Hyldemoer, Gnomes)
Spindle (*Earth*)	*Industry brings good results. You weave your own web of fate. Be careful of actions now that might affect your future.* (Three Faery Queens, Frau Holda).
Blackthorn (*Earth*)	*You are being attacked by adversity but are protected. The end of a phase is in sight. Focus on the good future ahead.* (Faery Godmother)
Beech (*Air*)	*The power of communication is yours. You have the strength and endurance to see*

projects through to the end.

(Ogma, Wishing Faeries)

Fir (*Air*)   *You have the gift of clear sight. A bright light illuminates your pathway. Spiritual awareness is strong.*

(Sylphs, King of Dwarfs)

Aspen (*Air*)   *Your intuition has a message of guidance for you. Others will listen to you. Meditation brings rewards from the Otherworld.*

(Faery Queen)

Cherry (*Air*)   *You have the strength of the warrior. Difficulties can be overcome. Nothing is as bad as you imagined.*

(Vilas)

Apple (*Water*)   *You have a feeling of wholeness. Be careful of being seduced by outside possibly life-changing influences. Do not be blinded to reality.*

(Queen of Elfland, Faery Maiden, Sirens, Undines)

Birch (*Water*)   *The birth of something is imminent. A new beginning that will grow and mature into something more substantial.*

(Gille Dubh)

Willow (*Water*)   *It is time for healing of the mind, spirit and body. You are blessed with inspiration. Sew the seeds now for the future.*

(Brigid of the Tuatha Dé Dannan)

Hazel (*Water*)   *You have the power to gain knowledge. New ideas abound and you have guidance. Wisdom will ensue, along with improvement.*

(Sinann of the Shannon, and Boann of

the Boyne Rivers)

Rowan (*Fire*)
You have magical protection allowing you to be more creative and outgoing. Objections will be overcome by your resilient strength. You have psychic and personal power.
(Dragon, Tuatha Dé Dannan, Diarmuid and Grainne)

Holly (*Fire*)
You need to recharge your personal battery. The return of the light will help you. The time of dormancy is over there is now hope for the future and plans can be made.
(Danu, Unicorn, The Holly King)

Alder (*Fire*)
The spring is nigh and regeneration is at hand. You can now take control. New or revived relationships are indicated. The doorway to a brighter future opens.
(The Phoenix, The Raven, Darker Faeries, Salamander)

Yew (*Fire*)
Something will die so rebirth can take place. New life either personally or spiritually will transpire. Changes will bring a new light and a new existence, so clear out the old.
(Etain, The Stag)

Elementals (Pos)
Wands become positive or enhanced.

Salamander (Neg)
Wands become negative.

Main Points

Tree	Element	Faery/Faeries	Offering	Contact
Oak (portal)	Fire	Dryad, Oakmen, Brigid, Dagda, Oak King	Coins, gemstones, jewelry, ribbons, snowdrops	Jupiter/ Thursday, Lughnasadh
Ash (portal)	Fire	Light Elves, Dark Elves (Dwarfs), Frost * and Fire Giants, Meliae	Incense, water, gemstones, small cakes, honey	Sun/Sunday, Samhain, Summer Solstice
Hawthorn (portal)	Fire	Queen of Elfland, All Faeries	Ribbons, gemstones, honey, small cakes	Mars/Tuesday, Bealtaine, Twilight
Elm	Earth	Light Elves, Dark Elves (Dwarfs)	Milk, mead, gemstones, flute	Saturn/ Saturday, Samhain
Elder (portal)	Earth with Water	Hyldemoer, Gnomes	Water, collect litter	Venus/Friday, Summer Solstice
Spindle	Earth	Three Faery Godmothers or Queens, Frau Holda	Ribbons, craft item, corn dolly	Christmas Eve – 12th Night, Winter Solstice/Yule, Lughnasadh, Wednesday or Friday

Blackthorn (portal)	Earth with Fire	Faery Godmother, Lunantishee	Fruit (berries, apples), ribbons, gemstones	Samhain, Bealtaine, Spring Equinox, Autumn Equinox, twilight, New Moon period
Beech	Air with Earth	Ogma, Wishing Faeries	Water, gemstones, small cakes	Saturn/ Saturday, Wednesday, Imbolg, New Moon
Fir	Air	Sylphs, King of Dwarfs	Feathers, incense, bubbles, gemstones	Imbolg, Spring Equinox, Bealtaine, Dawn, New Moon
Aspen	Air	Faery Queen	Drums, tinkling bells, or other percussion instrument	Spring/ Summer day, Bealtaine, Summer Solstice
Cherry	Air	Vilas	Small cakes, flowers, fruits, pretty objects	Venus/Friday, Spring Equinox

Apple	Water	Faery Maiden/ Queen of Elfland, Three Faery Queens, Sirens, Undines	Water, green gemstones	Venus/Friday, Samhain
Birch	Water	Gille Dubh	Ribbons, nuts, water	Venus/Friday, Bealtaine, Samhain
Willow	Water	Brigid	Ribbons, candles, spring water, primroses, mugwort	New Moon, Waxing Moon/ Monday, Imbolg
Hazel	Water	Sinann, Boann, Salmon, Melsh Dick, Churnmilk Peg (of Yorkshire)	Gemstones, ribbons, flowers	Mercury/ Wednesday, Autumn Equinox
Rowan	Fire	Dragon, Salamander, Brigid and the Tuatha Dé Danann, Diarmuid and Grainne	Red ribbons, gemstones, incense, candles	Sun/Sunday, All Celtic festivals but Bealtaine and Summer Solstice
Holly	Fire	Danu, Unicorn, Holly King	Red/green ribbon, candle	Saturn/ Saturday, Winter Solstice, Summer Solstice, Mars/Tuesday

Alder (portal)	Fire with much water	Darker Faeries, Phoenix, Salamander, Raven	Water, candles, red gemstones, garnet/ruby	Venus/Friday, Pisces, Mars/ Tuesday, Spring Equinox
Yew	Fire	Etain, Stag	Incense, gemstones (clear or white)	Saturn/ Saturday, New Moon, Samhain, Bealtaine, Imbolg, Spring Equinox

Celtic Wheel of the Year

There are eight festivals in the Wheel of the Year, four greater festivals, two solstices, and two equinoxes. They are magical times and therefore good times to contact faery. All Celtic festivals are celebrated from dusk of the eve of the day until the dusk of the following day (see Samhain).

Samhain

Samhain is celebrated on 31st of October (Southern Hemisphere this is 30th April) and is a greater festival. This celebration is also known as Hallowe'en or All Hallows Eve. As with all Celtic festivals it is celebrated from the eve of one day, which is dusk of October 31st until dusk the following day, 1st November.

In the Christian Calendar the 1st of November is All Saints Day (hence the name 'Eve of All Hallows' or Hallowe'en), and the 2nd is All Souls Day. This is occasionally recorded wrongly the other way around in books and websites. Hallow means 'to revere' or 'make holy' and the 1st of November has been dedicated to all saints, known and unknown, since the 8th century.

Samhain pronounced (sowin/sowen) is an important and major festival as it marks the end of the old year but at the same time the beginning of the New Year as the whole cycle begins again. It symbolizes rebirth in the midst of darkness.

This is a time for communication with spirit as the veil between our world and the Otherworld is thinned. As it is a *'tween time*, a time when it is neither the old year or the new, it is the night when the faery or sidhe are abound.

Winter Solstice/Yule

The Winter Solstice or Yule is on or about 21st of December (Southern Hemisphere this is 21st June). The Christian Church adopted this time of year to celebrate the birth of Jesus. Many customs, such as decorating a tree, hanging mistletoe and holly, and burning the Yule log, hark back to pagan days.

This is the shortest day of the year and the longest night, the end of the waning year and the beginning of the waxing year. From here on, the days once more become longer as the sun is reborn and we have the passage of darkness into light. This is a time for celebration and rejoicing as we emerge from the darkest months.

Evergreens are a wonderful decoration of this season of joy. They are the symbol of everlasting life in a world where all else is dormant, as well as of the undying sun. Holly is the most popular evergreen and wards off negativity.

It has been said that the Druids would cut Mistletoe from oaks with golden sickles and the branches were not allowed to touch the ground. They were used by the people as protection and hung over doorways. Hung over a baby's cradle it would also prevent the baby from being stolen by faeries (though this is not recommended now as the whole plant is poisonous).

The Oak King is a powerful giant figure of nature wearing oak foliage. He rules for the half year from the Winter Solstice until the Summer Solstice after defeating his twin brother the Holly King. The Oak king is the king of the light and the waxing year.

Imbolg

Imbolg is on 2nd February, (Southern Hemisphere is from dusk of the eve of 31st July) and is a greater festival and the winter festival of lights.

Imbolg (pronounced immolg) is also known as Imbolc, Oimelc, Candlemas, and in the US as Groundhog Day. This day is the day of triple Goddess Brigid or Bride (and other names) also a faery of the Tuatha Dé Danann. Her flower is the snowdrop and her white wand is made from birch. The Celtic Goddess Brigid is associated with the sun, fire, and water. It is said that immediately after she was born, a tower of flame burst from her forehead and reached from earth to heaven. She is a triple Goddess and patron of inspiration, poetry, midwifery, healing, the hearth, blacksmiths, arts and crafts, agriculture and husbandry.

As a saint, Brigid is the patron of Ireland, poets, dairymaids, blacksmiths, healers, cattle, fugitives, Irish nuns, midwives and new-born babies.

Imbolg is a time of cleansing and purification. The first signs of spring appear and the lambing season begins. Imbolg is a time for new beginnings, a time to spring clean, dispose of clutter, actual and mental, and begin afresh for the coming summer. Spring buds and flowers begin to appear.

A Brigid Cross is made from straw and is also known as a pagan sun wheel. It is woven in the center and has four radials which are tied at the ends. They were hung in the house for protection against fire. Many people still carry out this custom. On the eve of this festival a good fire was lit and Brigid was invited into the house to share in the celebrations.

Spring Equinox

The Spring Equinox, otherwise known as Eostara, is on or about 21st March (Southern Hemisphere this is 21st September). Eostara is a modern term for this festival, which is also known to some as Eostre and Ostara, after the Goddess Oestre, from which the term 'Easter' evolved.

This is a solar festival and a time of new life and balance as days and nights are equal. March is filled with optimism and the color yellow is all about us and reflected in daffodils, primroses and forsythia. They lift our spirits and remind us that as the sun becomes stronger, new growth and warm weather is in sight. Spring brings optimism, vitality, success, confidence and happiness. Buds appear on the trees too, and early spring blossom is in abundance, which makes it a lovely time for walking. Eggs hatch and new lambs are born. The egg symbolizes rebirth and fertility and is potential life, a very apt symbol for the time of year when everything begins to grow.

Bealtaine

Bealtaine on May 1st is a greater festival (Southern Hemisphere this is the 31st October from dusk onwards). Bealtaine, and meaning 'Bright fire' or 'Bel-fire', is also known as Beltane, and along with Samhain is considered to be the most important of the festivals. Bealtaine is associated with an old custom of lighting bonfires to protect cattle from witches. May Day is still celebrated in villages and towns all over the British Isles.

Fertility has returned to the land and is celebrated in great style. A wealth of customs accompany May Day. Dancing around the maypole (a phallic symbol), is in actual fact a fertility rite. Jumping the Bel-fire for various reasons of luck was, and still is, a tradition in some villages. Hawthorn, bluebells, pansies, dead nettle and primroses, are flowers you can find at this time. Bealtaine also marks the end of winter and the beginning of summer. Lighting a Bel-fire was an ancient tradition. In pagan Ireland the fire was lit upon Tara Hill by the king, and no one was allowed to light theirs before he had lit his. St Patrick scored a point for Christianity by lighting a fire on a hill a few miles from Tara before the king had time to light his, which must have caused some anger and frustration.

Bealtaine is a time to celebrate unions, a time to celebrate love, sexuality and fruitfulness.

Summer Solstice

The Summer Solstice is on or about 21st of June (Southern Hemisphere this is 21st December) and is also known by the modern term Litha. In mid-June the sun is now at its highest and summer is at its peak. Midsummer has long had magical connotations and faeries abound at this time. Shakespeare's *A Midsummer Night's Dream* springs to mind with Puck and the faeries at large in the forest and up to much mischief.

In opposition to the Winter Solstice, this time we have the longest day with the shortest night. The year will now go into its waning phase. Traditionally, Bonfires and solar wheels were lit at this time of festivity to celebrate the Sun God at his most powerful.

As this time of year it is usually warm, so it is good to celebrate outdoors. This is the time when the pagans and Druids, head off to Stonehenge and Avebury and other sacred sites to celebrate. The Summer Solstice is a time to give thanks for the bounty of the land, for water, for sunlight, and indeed for all the elements.

The earth is bountiful with an abundance of flowers and vegetables and is a time of enjoyment of what you are and what you have achieved. Celebrations take the form of singing and dancing to celebrate life, death, and regeneration. Nature is a continuous cycle of death and rebirth. The year now goes into its waning phase, but at Yule the sun will rise again, beginning the cycle once more.

The Holly King is a powerful giant figure of nature wearing holly foliage. He rules the half year from the Summer Solstice until the Winter Solstice (Yule). He is the king of darkness and the waning year.

Lughnasadh

Lughnasadh is on August 1st (Southern Hemisphere this is 2nd February) and is a greater festival in the Celtic calendar. Lughnasadh (pronounced loo-nas-uh) is also known as Lammas. On this day Lugh the solar God of light and fire, is honored. The corn mother is also honored and the celebrations are a reward after hard labor.

Some people celebrate at this festival, the symbolic slaying of the Corn God. Others agree that this happens at the second harvest in September. This is because most corn is harvested in late August through until late September and especially so in Europe.

However, in English terms 'corn' means kernel, and the word 'corn' referred to different cereals. Corn dollies too were or are actually made of different cereals and it appears they were constructed at the first harvest when most grains are harvested.

This is the time of year when summer is on the wane and the sun loses strength, but it is also the time to harvest. The fruit is ripening fast on the trees, and summer flowers are in abundance. Everything has come to a maturity, but will soon begin to fade again.

The Grain Mother symbolizes the abundance of the Earth Mother, She who is the great provider and preserver of life. From here on we rest and take time to contemplate all that we have achieved during the sun's active phase and let the seeds of new objectives take root for the future. We must also sacrifice our active outer energy, and look to the time of rest and of inner power.

Autumn Equinox

The Autumn Equinox is on or around 21st of September (Southern Hemisphere this is 21st March) and is also known as Harvest Home and by the modern term Mabon.

Day and night are in perfect balance again. The sun is about to enter the sign of Libra bringing balance and harmony. The sun's power is fast waning, darkness is increasing and winter is just around the corner. This is the time of the second or final harvest of remaining fruits, vegetables and crops, and a time to give thanks. Mabon is a celebration with themes of thanksgivings and balance. Celebration takes the form of feasting to gives thanks for a good harvest, which with the end of growth in the land, will help see us over the cold, dark winter months.

We are poised between light and dark, life and death. Once more the wheel has turned reminding us that time is not linear but circular. What is born, lives, and dies, is reborn and the cycle begins again. This is a time to reconcile opposites, and to restore balance in our lives.

We must not mourn the warm fertile, summer days of our lives, as there is still much to look forward to. This is a time of peace, calm, and slowing down. Gladly autumn brings rich color and a warmth of its own, as it also brings wisdom and maturity. As winter comes, we are ready for well needed rest and fond reflection.

Color Correspondences

White
Moon, purity, peace, truth, creativity, new ventures, divine inspiration, attracting positive energy, protection

Black
Protection, acceptance, change, grounding, banishing negativity, the shadow self

Gold
Sun, higher spirituality, happiness, attraction, luck, money, inner strength, creativity

Silver
Moon, secret dreams, intuition, clairvoyance, protection, goddess, astral energy

Blue
Water, empathy, peace, healing, harmony, honesty, wisdom, spiritual matters, communication, intuition, loyalty

Red
Fire, vitality, potency, energy, passion, love, sexuality, power, courage, survival, strength, motivation

Yellow
Air, sun, happiness, optimism, communication, luck, confidence, creativity, attraction, careers, imagination, success

Purple
Psychic awareness, clairvoyance, magic, spiritual energy and growth, dreams, astral projection, inner happiness, wisdom

Pink

Love, friendship, affection, fidelity, devotion, honor, health, family, binding

Green

Earth, Romantic love, healing, fertility, money, good luck, abundance, growth, beauty, harvest, agriculture

Orange

Confidence, optimism, ambition, success, strength, creativity, energy, stamina, career, goals, legal matters

Brown

Earth, home, practical matters, animal healing, endurance, harvest, lost objects, legal matters

Grey

Uncertainty, confusion, tiredness, neutrality, stalemate, both absorbing and repelling (as black and white blend)

Bibliography and Suggested Reading

Briggs, Katharine M, *A Dictionary of Fairies, Hobgoblins, Brownies, Bogies, and other Supernatural Creatures,* Penguin Books Ltd, (1977 edition).

Briggs, Katharine M, *The Vanishing People,* B.T. Batsford Ltd, (1978).

Callow, Edward, *The Phynodderree and Other Legends of the Isle of Man,* J. Dean & son, (1882).

Crossley-Holland, Kevin, *The Norse Myths, Gods of the Vikings,* Penguin Books Ltd, (1993).

Curran, Bob, *The Truth About the Leprechaun,* Wolfhound Press, (2000).

Douglas, Sir George, *Scottish Fairy and folk Tales,* A.L. Burt Company (1901).

Eason, Cassandra, *A Complete Guide to Faeries & Magical Beings,* Red Wheel/Weiser (2002).

Graves, Robert, *The White Goddess,* Faber & Faber, (1961 edition).

Gregor, Reverend Walter, Notes on The Folk-Lore of the North-East of Scotland, Elliot Scott (for the Folk-Lore Society, 1881).

Guest, Lady Charlotte, *The Mabinogion,* HarperCollins Publishers, (2000 edition).

Jennings, Pete & Sawyer, Pete, *Pathworking,* Capall Bann Publishing, (1993).

Keightley, Thomas, *The Fairy Mythology, Illustrative of the Romance and Superstition of Various Countries,* H.G. Bohn, (1870).

Lenihan, Eddie, with Green, Carolyn Eve, *Meeting the Other Crowd, The Fairy Stories of hidden Ireland,* Gill & MacMillan Ltd, (2003).

Moore, A.W. *The Folk-Lore of the Isle of Man,* Brown & Son, (1891), D. Nutt, (1891).